THE FREEDOM

T0126154

THE FREEDOM

SHADOWS AND HALLUCINATIONS IN OCCUPIED IRAQ

CHRISTIAN PARENTI

PHOTOGRAPHS BY TERU KUWAYAMA

THE NEW PRESS

NEW YORK
LONDON

Requests for permission to reproduce selections from this book should be mailed to:

Permissions Department,
The New Press, 38 Greene Street, New York, NY 10013

Published in the United States by The New Press, New York, 2004
Distributed by W. W. Norton & Company, Inc., New York

ISBN 1-56584-948-5 (hc.)
ISBN 1-59558-037-9 (pbk.)
CIP data available

The New Press was established in 1990 as a not-for-profit alternative to the large, commer-
cial publishing houses currently dominating the book publishing industry. The New Press
operates in the public interest rather than for private gain, and is committed to publishing,
in innovative ways, works of educational, cultural, and community value that are often
deemed insufficiently profitable.

www.thenewpress.com

Book design by Steven Hiatt

Printed in the United States of America

10 9 8 7 6 5 4 3 2 1

This book is dedicated to the people of Iraq

Contents

Preface

The *Freedom* does not provide a sweeping analysis of the war in Iraq. Instead, it offers a slice of political feeling and flavor, a snapshot of a time and place: Iraq during the first year of U.S. occupation. Of course, description always implies and slips into explanation, so this book is not without a point of view.

I have chosen descriptive reportage over a more analytic approach for a number of reasons. One is the surfeit of already existing radical analyses of the Iraq debacle and post–Cold War U.S. foreign policy in general. Add to that critical literature the rash of insider exposés and the shockingly blunt official arguments made by the Bush administration and elements in the pundit class *for* American domination of the globe, and there hardly seems to be much room for critique.

Writing and researching this book took a toll on the people closest to me; in particular, Heather Rogers was very dismayed at my return trips to the war zone. I am sorry for the stress I caused her. But despite that stress she read part of this manuscript and gave important editorial advice and support that made the book possible.

I am indebted to a number of other people. Foremost among them is Neil Smith, my boss at CUNY, who allowed me time off and tolerated my journalist detours away from my scholarly obligations. Without Neil's generosity, completing this book would have been extremely difficult. My publisher, Colin Robinson, was instrumental in getting *The Freedom* started and finished. Special thanks to Steve Hiatt, the most thorough and competent man in American publishing even in the face of high-speed deadlines. Betsy Reed at *The Nation,* where parts of this book first appeared as articles, was a superb and helpful editor. So too was Roane Carey. Thanks also to Katrina vanden Heuvel, who was supportive of my reporting from Iraq. Peter Garfield was generous in helping me edit my own photos, which were ultimately not used here. As for the photos that do grace these pages, I deeply appreciate the generosity, hard work and genius of Teru Kuwayama. Sarah Hughes at Corbis helped facilitate this link with Teru. During my last trip to Iraq, when I was dealing with the book deadline and the stresses that come with being in a war zone, she was a supportive friend with a cool head, warm heart and good Internet connection.

Logistics in Iraq can be difficult and morale there is hard to maintain. My trips there were greatly facilitated by the support, friendship and humor of Ahmed Ayad, Dahr Jamail, David Enders, Salam Talib, Jabran Y. Mansoor, Harb Mukhtar, Garrett Scott, Ian Olds, Scott Fleming, Rob Eshelman, Dave Martinez and Rick Rowley. I also owe thanks to the many friends who, sometimes unwittingly, offered insights, comment, contacts and encouragement. That list includes Mustafa Bayoumi, Naomi Klein, David Harvey, Doug Henwood, Liza Featherstone, John Marshal, Penny Lewis, Williams Cole, Ted Hamm, and Chris Reilly. Finally, thanks to all the people in Iraq—Iraqis and American soldiers—who trusted me and spoke openly and shared their experiences. Without their contributions this book would not exist.

Christian Parenti
Brooklyn, July 2004

Ah, the freedom. Look, we have the gas-line freedom, the looting freedom, the killing freedom, the rape freedom, the hash-smoking freedom. I don't know what to do with all this freedom.

Akeel, twenty-six, on life in the New Iraq

1

To Babylon

The belief in the possibility of a short decisive war appears to be one of the most ancient and dangerous of human illusions.

Robert Lynd, Irish essayist and nationalist

At a gas station deep in the desiccated wastes of western Iraq, a producer for Fox TV waits to meet his armed and flak-jacketed security entourage. The producer is a man in his mid-fifties named Frank, of medium height, good looking, fit, with closely cropped gray hair. He was in Vietnam with the US military, then went straight into television and spent the next thirty years "in the business." Friendly and confident, Frank wears just the right clothes: khaki cargo pants, charcoal fleece pullover, Gore-Tex windbreaker. He scans the lunar landscape and announces: "I think we're gonna have it all wrapped up by March."

It is December 2003, and Frank is talking about the chaotic little war gripping Iraq's so-called Sunni Triangle. This oil-stained refueling depot on Iraq's main east–west highway is the war's front gate. Beyond here things begin to get "hot," with thieving *Ali Babbas* and the armed resistance preying on civilian traffic and military convoys alike. Usually the anonymous gunmen are content just to loot the gear of TV journalists or empty the wallets of Iraqi and Jordanian sojourners, but sometimes it gets worse. In April 2004 the Halliburton subsidiary Kellogg, Brown & Root announced that eighty of its convoys had been attacked and more than thirty of its employees had been killed in the previous year.

About the time I met Frank, two contractors were gunned down, then a CNN crew was fired on, leaving two dead and two wounded; then an Arab news crew working for Reuters was stopped by resistance fighters just outside Falluja. Forced to lie facedown on the ground with guns to their heads and accused of being US collaborators, the reporters barely survived: they had committed the sin of chatting with American troops at a checkpoint. Quick talking and perhaps a little help from Allah got them back to Baghdad, shaken but alive.

The situation for US forces in these parts is exponentially more dangerous. In the first year of the occupation, American patrols were attacked an average of twenty times a day with roadside bombs, rocket-propelled grenades (RPGs), mortars or small arms fire. By the end of its first year in Iraq the United States had, according to the Pentagon, lost more than 700 killed in action with almost 4,000 wounded.

And after one year of occupation, Iraq—the birthplace of civilization— lies in ruins: occupied, violent, corrupt, improvised, chaotic, mildly radioactive, and stalked by a gathering storm of religious fundamentalism, irredentist nationalisms and criminal mayhem. As for Iraqi casualties, no official figures are available. But a freelance website in Europe, www. Iraqbodycount.net, uses press reports to keep a running tally, and at the one-year mark estimated that between 8,800 and 10,000 Iraqis had been killed and an unknown number wounded. Meanwhile, the Coalition Provisional Authority's jails and prisons have held an estimated 43,000 suspects, thousands of whom still float in a legal limbo somewhere between the laws of war and the nebulous legal codes of a future Iraq.

Frank from Fox TV looks out at the desert and sees little of this. Instead, he apprehends a political mirage: the idea of American imperial beneficence and competence. For him the conquest of Iraq, the war, the chaos, the Bush administration's ambitious, and openly stated, plans for global control are all part of an exciting drama in which the American national character is being put to the test. As in a movie this narrative has a clear structure: the initial challenge, the first easy victory, then the dramatic setback, the moment of doubt, followed by recovery, renewed resolve, and the inevitable final victory.

For a moment I can almost see it, too, reflected in Frank's slightly mirrored sunglasses and in that friendly American smile that invites me, his countryman, to join in and feel good, feel optimistic, feel noble, feel like a winner. But shift focus back from the screen above the empty horizon onto the more immediate surroundings and the narrative begins to unravel. The Iraq I found during parts of 2003 and 2004 was more like a half-repressed memory of abuse than a drama of hope and redemption. This mess was the joint product of Saddam Hussein's despotism and US conquest, the final phase of a long, slow-boiling war that started in 1991 with Operation Desert Storm, continued under the Clinton-era regimen of sanctions and occasional bombings, and moved into completion when the armies of George W. Bush marched on Baghdad.

To travel in central Iraq is to visit modernity's junkyard. Here one finds a traditional society that in a few short decades threw off British colonialism, embraced a semi-secular nationalism, grabbed its economic bootstraps, and, with the help of oil money, pulled itself out of underdevelopment in less than a generation. But now this project is unraveling and moving backward, or rather forward, into a dystopian future of poverty, crime and religious moralism. Looters continue to cannibalize the country's infrastructure; its markets are swamped by cheap imports; and in desperation ever more Iraqis are turning to the imagined virtues and traditions of a fundamentalist past that never really existed.

The Baath Party for all its faults was Iraq's primary builder of modernity. In control of the state the party constructed highways, canals, cement plants, universities, power grids and modern working-class housing. Saddam was central to all of this even before his 1979 coup against his al-Tikriti relative and mentor, President Ahmad Hassan al-Bakr. During the seventies, it was Saddam who ran the show and pointed the way forward while al-Bakr and the even more distant figure of Baath Party founder Michel Aflaq were reduced to figureheads. Saddam was a thug, but not a banana republic–style comprador, no mere tool of outside powers. Rather he was a classical fascist who used the party and state to build "the nation." The political economy of Baathist Iraq was that weird left–right combination of policies that has marked so much of post–Second World War development in the Global South.

Saddam's Iraq was a mixed economy, one in which the rentier state with its huge oil revenues both nurtured and disciplined the private forces of the market. In Baathist Iraq all that was solid did indeed melt into air: most of old Baghdad was torn down and replaced, and the "Great Leader," impatient with capitalism's slow march toward industrialization, used the state's political machinery—with all its terror, theatrics, grandeur and oil money—to drive development. At the heart of this endeavor was the Iraq Petroleum Company, nationalized in 1973. By these means Saddam built up a cadre of technocrats, cooperated with foreign capital, and developed agriculture, petrochemicals and manufacturing. In doing all of this he dragged much of the population away from rural tradition and into the light of prosperity, urbanization and cosmopolitanism.[1]

But the dictator's madness—his domestic terror, his monumental van-

ity and late-stage gluttony, which took the form of huge palaces and deca-
dent sons running their own fiefdoms—led to a plague of endless wars
that left his masterpiece worn down, in decline. First there was the war
with Iran, which began in September 1980 when Saddam, playing the part
of an ersatz Saladin, invaded his Persian neighbor. Nominally this was to
settle a border dispute, but in reality the war was an opportunistic move
against the newly consolidated religious revolution in a weakened Iran.
Like many other massive military blunders, this war was supposed to end
in a quick, decisive victory. But the Ayatollah Ruhollah Khomeini, using the Shah's old military hardware and officer corps, fought back hard,
blocking Iraqi ships from using the Persian Gulf and opening a counterattack that devastated Iraq's main oil facilities at Fao.

Soon Iraq was going broke, burning up its $30 billion in foreign ex-
change reserves in the first two years of the war and borrowing billions
more. Before long it had ceased all imports other than food and weaponry. This is how *Time* magazine described Iraq's plight: "The government
is so hard up that it conducts a form of national telethon soliciting money
and gold for the war effort. Every night on TV, a newscaster reads off the
names of the latest contributors, while some of the donors are shown
gazing at their donations."[2]

On the front with Iran the fighting settled into a World War I–style
stalemate where each side bombarded the other's lines, then attacked the
opposing trenches in horrific slaughters that resulted in little or no progress for either army. The war's political and economic fallout brought
OPEC to its knees by undermining the cartel's unity and forcing the fi-
nancially desperate belligerents to overproduce oil, thus lowering prices,
which led to more overproduction, and then even lower prices, and so
on in a vicious cycle. By the end of the war in July 1988, Iraq, with the
second-largest oil reserves in the world, owed $40 billion to international

creditors.³ An estimated 400,000 people died in the carnage, with up to 750,000 wounded; the majority of these casualties were Iranian.⁴

Stoking the inferno from behind the scenes were the US and its regional vassal Saudi Arabia, thanks to the deft intermediary work of Saudi Prince Bandar, aka Mr. Smoothy in D.C. diplomatic circles. Though Saddam had links with the CIA dating back to his 1959 assassination attempt on the reformist President Qasim, he built closer ties to the US during his war against Iran. At that time Washington saw a strong Iraq as a bulwark against Iran and as protection for the Saudi royal family, which sat on an ocean of oil and ruled a restive Shiite minority.

As Craig Unger explains, Washington's infatuation with Saddam went as far as providing him with the tools to make weapons of mass destruction: "Beginning in 1984, the Center for Disease Control began providing Saddam's Iraq with biological materials—including viruses, retroviruses, bacteria, fungi and even tissue that was infected with bubonic plague." Two years later the Reagan administration authorized the Saudis to send Iraq 1,500 MK-84 bombs (the same sort the US would later use on Iraq). Ultimately, the Reagan administration gave Iraq more than $5 billion in loan guarantees, and these funds, along with other aid, enabled Saddam "to become a major military force in the Persian Gulf," one that did for a while in the late eighties and early nineties have chemical and nuclear weapons programs.⁵

Then in the summer of 1990 Saddam turned on Kuwait in an effort to recoup both his financial and his political losses. The "Hero Leader" accused the emirate of "slant drilling" into the Rumaila oil fields on the Iraq–Kuwait border. (Pressure in the fields had dropped and Saddam's accusations may well have had merit.) The dictator demanded cancellation of Iraq's $7 billion war debt to Kuwait. The emirate refused to pay, and on August 2, 1990, Saddam's army conquered and occupied its neighbor.⁶

It is said that Saddam's original plan was only to take the disputed oil fields, but that at the last minute, thinking that he had tacit US approval, he decided to take the rest of Kuwait as well.

Iraqi nationalists from King Faisal to the Baathists had long claimed Kuwait as a lost province. And the United States had supported Saddam's wing of the Baath Party in its 1963 and 1968 coups d'état. As late as December 1983 Donald Rumsfeld, acting as President Reagan's special envoy to the Middle East, met Saddam to discuss a westbound oil pipeline through Jordan to the port of Aquba. At that point Saddam had already used chemical weapons against Iranian troops. Rumsfeld said nothing about these crimes. Thus in 1990 Saddam's faith in US support for his invasion of Kuwait was not unwarranted.

Instead, the response was America's Operation Desert Storm, a war that killed at least 100,000 Iraqi soldiers and civilians and left Iraq with more ruined infrastructure, more onerous war debts, and more reparations to pay. The defeat was followed by twelve years of brutal sanctions. Some were imposed by the United Nations and managed from an office in New York that governed the sale of oil and the importation of food and medicine. Another regime of sanctions was imposed unilaterally by the United States under the Iraq Sanctions Act of 1990. This embargo included a broad array of "dual-use" items that were vital to running the Iraqi electrical and water systems and a modern economy in general. The list included high-speed computers, heavy-duty trucks, boilers, turbines, pumps, compressors, cables and transformers. In the north and south, Iraq's skies were policed by American and British fighter jets. From these "no-fly zones" the allies launched continuous low-level punitive bombing raids, taking out a radar facility here, a communications post there, often leaving a few dead soldiers or technicians in the rubble.

As a result of all this, public investment broke down, industrial production declined, and cultural production stagnated. For example, film production, a measure of national investment in the arts, stopped completely, while the death rate among Iraqi children under the age of five, a leading social indicator, increased from 56 deaths per thousand live births to 131 deaths per thousand in 1994–99. UNICEF has estimated that up to half a million Iraqi children died because of the sanctions regime.[7]

War and sanctions left Iraq's project of development and modernization in crisis. Then in 2003 came the coup de grâce: Bush Jr. sent his armies to Baghdad in a quick and bloody three-week rollover. It is upon this heap of wreckage and corpses that the current drama in Iraq unfolds.

The trip into Iraq, like so many details of the occupation, encapsulates the crisis and ruin of the larger whole. In early August 2003, I left from Amman at five in the morning. Typically one joins a convoy of two or three GMC Suburbans—for some reason these sturdy SUVs are the vehicle of choice on the Amman-to-Baghdad route, but I have also done the trip in an orange Chevy Caprice taxicab. The Suburbans depart through the dark and empty streets of Amman, then head down to Highway 10, a beat-up two-lane ribbon of tarmac that stretches east some 250 kilometers into a desert that is alternately flat or gently rolling but always densely littered with jagged, dark volcanic rocks the size of eggplants and pumpkins. Sitting on the desert surface the rocks give the terrain an implausible appearance, as if the debris had been dumped from the sky only months ago. At other points the scene looks like a massive rock farm or a gentle swelling sea of floating black stones. Through these rockfields have been cleared pathways the width of a truck's axle. So barren and harsh is the landscape that it is hard to imagine how the Bedouins who still traverse these plains manage to feed their herds of goats and sheep. Today the desert nomads often drive high-wheeled Mercedes trucks with long flat beds built up with wooden sides in which they haul animals, spare gas and other gear. When not rolling slowly through the desert, the Bedouins graze their sheep and goats and camp in low woolen tents.

After the sea of rocks, the desert gives way to an even more empty and dusty landscape, and then one arrives at the border. There are already signs of trouble as one leaves the Hashimite Kingdom of Jordan. In the quarter-mile-wide "no man's land" between the two border crossings to the left and right of the highway are the small tent cities of the al-Ruwayshid refugee camp, home to over 1,000 Palestinians and some Iranian Kurds who are stranded in an international void, a legal non-place, between the borders of Jordan and American-occupied Iraq. The refugees, who fled the US invasion on temporary travel documents, or were deported from Iraq during the buildup to war, are mostly women, children and the elderly; one report mentioned 500 minors. They have been demanding return to their original countries or the right to go back to Baghdad, but the US and Jordan do not oblige.[8]

Passing by the wind-whipped camp in August I saw their hand-painted English and Arabic signs demanding aid and repatriation. When we slowed to take photographs armed Jordanian border guards adamantly shooed us away. It was a bad omen. The ubiquitous Peter Kessler, spokesman for the UN High Commissioner for Refugees, made some noises about this floating population and its need for medical care.[9] But six months later the refugee camp was still there, an inconsequential blip on the screen in a region that seems more violent and unstable each week.

After minimal hassle at the Iraqi border and a chat with a few of the GIs who sometimes search vehicles, sometimes just sit around, the convoys of big GMC SUVs race toward Baghdad. In Iraq the highway and the desert together looks like southeastern California or Nevada: the land is dry and flat, the road well paved, wide with divided lanes and familiar metal guardrails. This is the Autobahn of Saddam's Arab Reich. The good road allows steady speeds of up to 105 miles an hour, except when detouring around a bombed-out bridge or the occasional wrecked vehicle. The flattened frame of one car is said to be the remains of one of Uday Hussein's Ferraris that was "borrowed" by one of his unlucky associates in a failed attempt to flee American air strikes. A colleague would later muse comically about hiring someone to haul it to Basra so we could ship it off in a cargo container and sell it on EBay. The second time I went in, the wreck was gone.

Though I heard a credible report of an SUV being accidentally strafed by a US helicopter, the only really dangerous part of the drive is the section from Ramadi past Falluja to the edge of Baghdad. During this leg drivers become visibly nervous—most of them say they've been robbed. They push the heavy Suburbans into tight formations, running them side by side to block the highway with a speeding barricade to prevent gun-wielding *Ali Babbas* from overtaking. And though one's chances of being robbed are slim it is at these moments that all the secondhand stories come racing back, all the narrow misses, the images of friends of friends with guns to their heads.

On this route one arrives in Baghdad just as the sun is setting. The city opens ahead like a hallucination, a splendid, sprawling mess of flat, sand-colored homes, dry palms, Mussolini-style public monuments in traffic roundabouts and funky, late-seventies-style tower blocks. The air is punishingly hot and dry; the horizon reveals a shroud of suffocating smog. Instead of the endless straight path of the highway and the strange serenity of a day sealed in an SUV speeding through the empty gray-brown desert, the city at sunset is vibrant with muddy orange detail. Now one swerves and loops, sharing the streets with cars, donkey carts, trucks and US tanks. To the side are flat buildings, shaggy bushes, and tall, dirty palm trees; then street stalls, pedestrians, taxis and a district of shops, all interspersed with bombed-out or looted buildings housing heaps of garbage and packs of stray dogs.

In times past Baghdad was considered the great summit of Arab and Islamic culture. An early example of urban planning, the city was laid out in a circle favored with fountains, gardens and the shade of looming palms, all fed by the mighty Tigris River curving through the city's heart. Mecca and Medina might be Islam's spiritual points of origin, but Baghdad has always been Arab Islam's cultural center: it was the seat of the great Abbasid Empire, Islam's first world power, which survived from 700 AD to the mid twelfth century. Abbasid Baghdad was a multicultural world where Christianity and Judaism as well as other minor cults were treated with tolerance. This dialogic stance allowed intellectual crossfertilization and served as an epistemological framework for flourishing international trade, which led to Islamic inventions such as long-distance banking and finance. Islam's separation of faith and reason, and the city's diversity, allowed law, science, art and trade to flourish. Ancient Greek knowledge was preserved, as were ideas from India and China, all while Europe stagnated through the Dark Ages of warlordism, ignorance and book-burning Catholic fanaticism. It's a history well known to the proud Baghdadis.

More recently Baghdad has been marked by a fascistic cult of order and planning; wide boulevards, parks, roundabouts, statues, grand monuments and highway overpasses set the tone. It is the urban geography of oil money. Today Baghdad is a sprawling, increasingly ramshackle metropolis of four million people, most of them unemployed and many of them armed.

The city's air is nightmarishly bad. On the horizon, looming above the date palms and low-rise residential sprawl, is a set of giant smokestacks; one belches a massive black plume (an Iraqi engineer told me that this is the result of burning petroleum by-products rather than natural gas or oil). Add to this the haze of smoldering garbage heaps, the stench of ruptured and backed-up sewers, and the ubiquitous dust from building rubble and frequent sandstorms, then cap and seal the mixture with the 115-degree hostility of the fierce desert sun. Or, if it's winter, mix this aerosol stew with a thick chilly river fog. Either way the air is almost unbreathable.

Crossing the Jumhuriyah Bridge in the center of Baghdad, the view suddenly opens on both sides and below is the wide Tigris River. At first glance the river and the city on its banks look strangely familiar. The point of reference soon becomes apparent: crossing the Tigris from west to east on the Jumhuriyah presents a view that is uncannily similar to crossing the Thames from south to north on the Waterloo or Blackfriars Bridges: the river's width, its placid, murky surface, the long, slow arch of its bow from left to right, the spacing and size of the buildings on the riverbanks, all look familiar. But in this apocalyptic version of London the sky has been transformed from leaden gray to the burning brilliance of a smog-filtered sunset, and the Houses of Parliament and Big Ben have been replaced by futuristic petroleum-funded trophy architecture: stunning slabs and towers of poured concrete with hanging balconies and cantilevered outcroppings, beautiful but charred and hollow. The last bit of robust forward-looking optimism in these structures was stripped away, along with the furniture, wiring and pipes, by the hordes of impoverished looters who followed in the path of the US takeover like locusts.

Across the river and down among the side streets, life appears normal but the mood bristles with tension. Crime is rife, electricity is in short supply, and even water flows erratically. Garbage and sewage fester on empty lots. Prices are soaring as wages stagnate. The nights echo with gunfire. Traffic is infuriatingly congested thanks to the roadblocks on major arteries, powerless traffic lights, and wave after wave of duty-free imported cars. Cement blast barriers and coils of sharp concertina wire are everywhere. Fuel shortages are common and the lines of cars waiting hours—and sometimes even days—for gas stretch for up to a mile, snarling traffic even more. The basic infrastructure is still in tatters. One of the city's main water treatment plants received a direct hit from American bombing, and several others were damaged by twelve years of sanctions that limited importation of vital spare parts; still other plants were ravaged by looters, who stole computers, tore out pipes and ripped up cables.

A city without adequate water, power and safety, a city forced to live in its own wastes, is a breeding ground for violence, despair and, in this case, theocratic revolution.

2

Fear City, Capital of Chaos

Once you've got Baghdad, it's not clear what you do with it. It's not clear what kind of government you would put in place of the one that's currently there... How much credibility is that government going to have if it's set up by the United States military when it's there? ... I think to have American military forces engaged in a civil war inside Iraq would fit the definition of quagmire, and we have absolutely no desire to get bogged down in that fashion.

Secretary of Defense Dick Cheney,
April 29, 1991

On the streets below Baghdad's high-rise ruins, chaos and fear reign. Saddam emptied the prisons in October 2002 and in May of the next year L. Paul Bremer III fired the police and disbanded the army but allowed the citizenry to keep their Kalashnikov assault rifles; in the capital people are allowed to own one machine gun, one pistol and one antique firearm per household. (When Falluja was under US control, the rule there was only one gun.)

In occupied Iraq the criminal is king, while fear and growing hopelessness corrode the social fabric. Drivers get executed for their vehicles; girls are snatched up and gang-raped, while the wealthy live in constant fear of ransom-seeking kidnappers. Sixty percent of Iraqis are out of work. Guns, sex and pharmaceuticals flood the underground economy: a thousand Valium tablets costs less than five dollars in most pharmacies. During the summer of 2003 a friend of mine was offered hand grenades for three dollars apiece in Falluja. Bizarrely, the background music to this madness is the lilting and dignified Arabic verse of the five daily calls to prayer.

The crew I am with on my first trip in consists of the filmmaker Garrett Scott and a Bay Area lawyer-cum-writer Scott Fleming. Through another filmmaker, James Longley, we've linked up with a translator named Akeel. He's tall and thickset, almost heavy, with a shaved head, wraparound shades, hip goatee and a goofy sense of humor that belies his hard-man persona. In many ways he is a big kid, with a head full of pop culture references and fantasies of the perfect girl. But he is also deeply nationalistic. (Akeel has asked that I not use his last name in this book.) As my colleagues and I unload our gear, two men drive by our cheap hotel flashing small submachine guns. Forty minutes later nervous American soldiers from the 1st Armored Division move in looking for "bad guys." Heading out for breakfast the next morning we find three big plain-clothes Iraqi cops (some of the few then on the job) beating and interrogating a suspect in the lobby of our hotel. With their pistols drawn the cops turn and smile politely as we pass out of view, then the beat-down continues. The bound and thumb-tied perp is an accused kidnapper. When stage one of "questioning" is over the battered detainee is loaded into the trunk of a Chevy Impala and driven away. This is liberated Baghdad: an endless game of cops-and-robbers with loosely improvised rules.

No accurate crime statistics are kept here, so journalists go to the morgue for numbers—at least they did until the Coalition Provisional Authority, wishing to project a more stable image, put pressure on the city morgue to keep its doors shut. According to the morticians there were 470 known murders in July 2003, up from 10 the year before. (Dictatorial police states have their compensations.) In August, 518 Baghdadis were killed with firearms. But many Iraqis, fearful of the authorities and observant of the Muslim tradition requiring a quick burial, don't bother to bring their dead to morgues to be counted, so no one knows the real number of crimes.[1] And not all "authorities" keep statistics.

In the slum of Sadr City—which was once called al-Thawra (The Revolution), then Saddam City, and is now named for the father of the thirty-one-year-old "outlaw" Shiite cleric, Muqtada al-Sadr—Shiite militias keep order on the streets and maintain a network of private jails. The main force in this impoverished sprawl of cinder-block homes and jerry-rigged wires running from house to house is the Mahdi Army, or Jeshi Mahdi, loyal to Muqtada al-Sadr. The force is named after Shia Islam's once and future twelfth caliph or "chosen one"—the Mahid. Al-Sadr's para-state activities take place off the books; journalists don't get stats on the number of rapes, robberies and murders cleared by the Mahadi, so it's impossible even to guess the real crime rate in Baghdad.

More generally, Iraq's legal system is now a patchwork of negotiable codes, customs and political favors. Bribery and nepotism are rife. Tribes and courts compete for legitimacy; police officers are often clan sheikhs and in that capacity moonlight as community mediators or informal judges, arbitrating disputes and presiding at informal tribal courts called fassels. These gatherings handle cases, such as murder, that in any functioning state would fall within the criminal code. One press account described a deal in which a killing was resolved by means of a cash payment of several thousand dollars. The fassels' mix of Bedouin custom and Koranic teaching could be seen as a model of dialogical or restorative justice, but that would obscure important questions of unfairness based on

gender, class and social prestige. One Shia sheikh told me that his grandmother as a young woman was given to the family of the murderers of
her brother so that the two feuding families could "make a new person"
to replace the dead man. Amid the chaos of occupation this traditional
mistreatment of women is making a comeback. Ironically, Iraq is home
to what was probably the first written legal code: the sixth king of Baby-
lon, Hammurabi, wrote down national laws sometime around 1700 BC.[2]

By the late winter of 2003 there was (on paper) a force of 60,000 new
Iraqi police officers in the country; only about 4,000 of these patrolled
Baghdad and most of them stayed in the central areas, leaving the outer
neighborhoods to their own devices. The IP's job is rough: statistically
speaking they have one of the most dangerous occupations in the world.
Their casualty rate has been consistently higher than that of the American occupying forces. During the joint Sunni-Shiite Intifada of spring
2004 an estimated 10 to 30 percent of the cops in Shia areas of the south
switched sides or stayed away from the fighting.

As for crime, the US troops—the *kuwat al-ihtilal*, or forces of occupation—are stretched too thin to provide law and order. Beyond that,
the US military has little understanding of Iraqi culture or politics; many
soldiers arrive with minds freighted with orientalist notions of Arabs as
backward sheepherders in need of a firm guiding hand. As one army captain explained to the *New York Times*, "You have to understand the Arab
Mind… The only thing they understand is force—force, pride and saving
face."[3] Iraqis hate this sort of arrogance, and the more of it they see the
more they hate the occupation. As one highly educated and bilingual Iraqi
told me, "The Americans think we are Indians and a that this is the Wild
West." Another Iraqi, the relative of someone killed at a US checkpoint,
asked rhetorically why the US soldiers always used such strange names
like "Camp War Eagle" or "Task Force Panther," then offered his own

explanation: "It shows that they do not respect us, that they hate us."

When US troops do mean well they face the almost impenetrable barrier of language. Both soldiers and the civilian staff of the occupation are very short on Arabic language skills. The Bush administration and the military brass keep quiet about this issue, but former diplomats and intelligence officers worry openly about the language gap. Former US ambassador to Saudi Arabia Charles W. Freeman, now of the Middle East Policy Council, has likened the situation in Iraq to "a badly managed Pentagon-operated theme park," adding that, as of October 2003, only fifty-four Foreign Service officers were fluent in Arabic. He estimated that a similar number of case officers in the "intelligence community" also spoke Arabic. The ambassador pointed out that this leads to "communication problems."[4]

At crime scenes US troops can just as easily arrest the victims as the perpetrators. A human rights worker told me the story of a beauty shop that was attacked and robbed; some of the women were almost kidnapped. When the US troops showed up and were met by a small crowd of hysterical Baghdadis the soldiers were about to arrest some of the victims and witnesses until a bilingual Al-Jazeera reporter intervened and translated.

Not surprisingly, most people in Baghdad are armed and edgy. Under such conditions community solidarity takes on increasingly violent forms. An Irish peace activist, Michael Birmingham, who works for Voices in the Wilderness, a peace and human rights group that has tried to document and "witness" the misery of Iraq for almost a decade, saw the new vigilantism firsthand. Three carjackers took a vehicle at gunpoint in midday. In response, pedestrians started throwing stones at the thieves; shopkeepers started firing AK-47s, disabling the vehicle; then the crowd surged in, dragging one of the carjackers onto the street and beating him.

"They were jumping on his head and his chest. I don't think he made it," explained Birmingham in a deadpan Dublin brogue. Birmingham was himself beaten by a mob around the same time while he was watching a protest outside the Palestine Hotel where unemployed workers were demanding jobs. The assault was brief and he eventually escaped down an alley.

The staff of a youth-run newspaper, *Al-Muajaha,* tell similar stories. The paper shared space with Voices in the Wilderness in that group's bare, two-story cement offices and apartments just off Karrada Street. On some of the hottest August afternoons I'd sit around with these young, broke reporters waiting for the electricity to come back while listening to their tales of horror about who among their friends had been robbed or attacked; two people's relatives had been killed in carjackings.

Ahmed, a young dental technician turned press fixer and driver who worked with friends of mine, told a story of how his brother was kidnapped and held for $100,000. After the family paid almost $30,000 the boy was freed; then the entire family, except Ahmed, fled to Syria without saying a word to the police.

During the Intifada of April 2004 there was a rash of kidnappings against journalists, and many of these detained reporters lied about their nationalities and then did not report their detentions so as to keep working in Iraq. Before that journalists were getting whacked intentionally, and unintentionally killed in the crossfire. There was the Reuters cameraman, Mazan Dana, who was shot and killed by US troops outside the massive Abu Ghraib prison. In early July 2003 a young British freelancer, Richard Wild, was murdered by a lone assassin who probably thought his tall, broad-shouldered victim was a soldier. A Cambridge graduate who had served in the British army, Wild wanted to be a war correspondent. After only two weeks of freelancing he was dead. Word on the street that summer was that Wild had been wearing shorts and had spoken to US troops in front of the natural history museum just before he was shot execution-style in the base of the skull with a small-caliber weapon. Three GIs in the area had recently died the same way: at close range, in the neck, from behind, with a pistol. Wild had been staying with Birmingham and the other Voices in the Wilderness activists. When I visited Birmingham only three weeks after Wild's death the tragedy already seemed far away since every day brought new assaults and kidnappings.

Barely a month after Wild was murdered, May Ying Welsh, a stellar American reporter who then worked for Al-Jazeera, was almost killed while interviewing US soldiers. Standing on the second-floor atrium of the Coalition Provisional Authority's Convention Center, beneath a gaudy Baathist mosaic that depicts American cruise missiles raining down on Iraq along with doves and someone who looks like Saddam but is dressed like Saladin, May recounted her experiences with an air of blank serenity. She was doing a story on a Muslim GI who was on a humanitarian mission handing out books.

"The whole thing was something set up between Al-Jazeera and the 1st AD," explained Welsh. "The story was going fine until in the middle of an interview a grenade dropped right in between us like a ripe piece of fruit. Everyone ran, but I have this really bad habit of freezing when things get dangerous. So I just froze."

The grenade rolled under a Humvee, and the shrapnel somehow missed Welsh when it blew. "I think I was behind the tire," she says, taking a long drag on her cigarette. Her film crew and the two GIs she had been talking to were not so lucky: all were wounded, one badly.

The Baghdad offices of the Iraqi Workers Communist Party were, for several months after the conquest, housed in the remains of a looted bank near the base of the Jumhuriyah Bridge, just across the Tigris from the Coalition Provisional Authority's massive fortified "Green Zone," which occupies the grounds of Saddam's old Republican Palace.

The bank is bare, stripped to the naked brick by looters. First they took all the money, then all the equipment and furniture, then they ripped out the marble paneling, light fixtures, doorframes, windows, wiring, pipes and floor tiles. The bank is now shared by three interrelated organizations: the Workers Communist Party of Iraq, the Unemployed Union of Iraq and the Organization for Woman's Freedom in Iraq. Upstairs two homeless families squat in some of the rooms and the Party has a little one-room radio station.

To keep out the hostile militants of Muqtada al-Sadr's Mahdi Army, the Party and the UUI post armed guards. Just inside the bank's front door sit two young men in sandals, slacks and loose shirts. Kalashnikov rifles lie across their laps. They smile politely at passing guests and comrades but keep a watchful eye on the infernally hot noonday street outside. As we pull up to the bank some scavengers nearby exit the bomb-ventilated burned-out shell of a once sleek modernist office tower across the street. They load long strips of aluminum into a waiting minivan and drive off. The scene feels simultaneously apocalyptic and totally prosaic.

In a cool dark room toward the back of the stripped bank I meet Yanar Mohammed, head of the Organization for Women's Freedom in Iraq and a member of the Workers Communist Party of Iraq. She is meeting with activists from out of town, middle-aged, middle-class women wearing sensible, modest clothes. They look like librarians. On the metal desk in front of Mohammed is a laptop computer; her guests sit in plastic outdoor chairs like those that fill the restaurant patios. Across the cheap carpet extension cords run to a generator out back.

"We want a secular, democratic Iraq where women are full members of society," explains Mohammed after the visiting delegation leaves. A self-professed "ex-Muslim," Mohammed scorns the veil and is defiantly beautiful. She's in her mid forties with long black hair and intense eyes, and the top few buttons of her tight denim shirt are unfastened to reveal just a hint of cleavage. In the face of Iraq's brutal misogyny, her presentation of self is not flirtation so much as it is politically combative. Her look semaphores female agency, secularism and a desperate hope. The death threats are constant. When she travels the streets, bodyguards go with her. Mohammed has already faced several abduction attempts.

How did she get to this place? Mohammed explains that for years she was a refugee from Saddam's regime, living in Toronto and working as an architect designing high-rise condos. "I saw my husband taken off to war every three years. Our lives were being destroyed. I had to leave Iraq." In Toronto she hooked up with the IWCP's Canadian branch, and when the American conquest was wrapping up in mid-April she and her comrades rushed back to Iraq to start organizing the revolution. They launched the only feminist newspaper in Iraq, *Almosawat* (Equality), and slowly recruited members.

Yanar Mohammed explains that the class suffering most routinely, horribly and silently under the new regime of chaos is women. She tells me of marauding men in "misery gangs" that kidnap and rape women and girls at will. Some of these victims are dumped back on the streets only to be executed by their "disgraced" male relatives in what are called "honor killings." Many women and girls stay locked inside their homes for weeks at a time for fear that they will be assaulted on the street or because male relatives will not allow them to go out. Increasingly those who do venture out wear veils, since the misogynist ravings of the more fundamentalist clerics have warned that women who do not wear the *hejab* should not be protected.

"Unlike western feminists we put the liberation of women in the context of class liberation," explains Mohammed. The Party in turn sees the liberation of women as the central catalyst for class revolution in the Middle East. "In some ways gender in Iraq is like race in America. But the condition of women has been deteriorating. In the fifties and sixties, my mother wore sleeveless shirts and walked at night along the river here. Young women wore skirts, all the western fashions, had jobs, went out at night together without men," says Mohammed. "This current situation, this fundamentalism, is not natural, it is not even traditional. It is desperate and reactionary."

Iraq's war on women started well before the US occupation. During the conflict with Iran, Saddam invoked religion and patriarchy with greater frequency as things at the front fell apart. After his defeat and expulsion from Kuwait in 1991, the "Hero Leader" began to abandon the discourse of Arab nationalism and turn toward Political Islam for a new set of rhetorical props with which to reinvigorate the theater of state. In the late 1990s this took the form of the so-called *al-hamla al-Imaniya* or "faithfulness campaign" in which, Mohammed says, over 200 women in Baghdad and Mosul were accused of immorality, dragged from their homes, and beheaded in the streets by Saddam's Fedayeen—a sort of paramilitary shock troop of Baathist blackshirts, young suicide fighters and thugs responsible for fanatical forms of intimidation and moral hygiene. It was during this campaign that Saddam added the words *Allahu Akbar*—"God Is Great"—to the Iraqi flag, which bore the Arab nationalist and Islamic color scheme of red and black bands across the top and bottom and a white band in between with three green stars. He also incorporated some of the more backward elements of Iraq's tribal code into the country's broader legal code, which Mohammed says encouraged so-called "honor killings." With the crisis of occupation the patriarchal violence has grown worse. And so Yanar Mohammed and her comrades attack head on.

Honor killing is their top grievance. The UN Commission for Human Rights has reported that more than 4000 Iraqi women have been murdered in this way since 1991.[5] The OWFI says some victims were as young as thirteen and fourteen, murdered by uncles and brothers after being raped. According to Mohammed, scores of other teenagers have killed themselves to escape forced marriages. The Organization for Women's Freedom claims that it has saved 250 women who were threatened with honor killing by spiriting the intended victims away to new homes or temporary shelter.

From 1998 to 2000, the OWFI, together with its parent organization the Trotskyist-oriented Workers Communist Party of Iraq, operated a women's shelter in the semi-autonomous region of Iraqi Kurdistan. Since the end of the Gulf War, Iraqi Kurdistan has functioned as a de facto mini-state run jointly by two rival parties, the Patriotic Union of Kurdistan (PUK) and its sibling the Kurdistan Democratic Party (KDP). Seeking refuge in the north was an established practice; the mainline Communist Party did the same thing.

While in Kurdistan Mohammed's comrades set up a shelter for women threatened with honor killings. But Mohammed says the party ran afoul of the local "Peshmerga," or Kurdish guerrillas of the PUK. "They said we were teaching women to go against society. They banned our party and shut the shelter," says Mohammed. "The PUK is very reactionary—it allows and even supports honor killings."

The PUK denies these charges, but both Kurdish parties have well-established reputations as corrupt, brutal and politically shallow. Most institutions in Kurdistan are absurdly duplicated so that both parties can have a piece of the aid game. During August of that first summer other issues on Mohammed's mind are the threats from al-Sadr's Mahdi Army, which had recently ejected the Party from its offices in Najaf, and the survival of her organization's newspaper, *Almosawat*. She worries that the Coalition forces might shut them down, as has happened to other anti-American papers. At the end of our long interview Mohammed sums up: "Our demands are simple: No veiling. No sexual apartheid. Shelter for women."

There are other pieces of a secular Left in Iraq, but not many. The most prominent is the old, formerly Soviet-oriented Iraqi Communist Party. Once the largest communist party in the Middle East and the second largest party in Iraq, the ICP sent cadre to Kurdistan in the late sixties, where the mountains and the Peshmerga shielded them. The ICP always had a large number of Baghdadi Kurds in its ranks, and this helped its militants to acclimate to life in the north.

Yanar Mohammed and other leftist critics of the Iraqi Communist Party condemn it for collaborating with the occupation by taking a seat on the US-appointed Governing Council of Iraq. Mohammed says that the ICP's long association with the blunt nationalism of the Kurdish parties has had the effect of watering down the Party's politics from revolutionary to mildly reformist.

As part of my search for signs of a hopeful Iraqi future, I visit officials and members of the ICP on several occasions. The Party puts on a brave face, but it is an institution marked by deep trauma. Saddam killed and tortured to death thousands of communists—that, after all, was why the CIA backed his clique within the Baath Party during its 1963 and 1968 coups d'état.

"We are coaxing back the old members. The survivors are rebuilding," explains Mufid Jazairi, one of the party's Baghdad leaders. He won't tell me how many members the party has, but he claims that it has always been and still is very popular in Iraq. But most of the survivors I see are gray-haired urban professionals. In reality, the young excluded and working masses follow the simple message and green flag of Islam.

The political traction of Islam can be seen everywhere, perhaps most obviously in the increasing number of women wearing the *hejab* or headscarf. This trend started during the war with Iran and continued through the first war with the United States and into the sanctions regime. Now it is almost *de rigueur*, the sure sign of a society in deep crisis. More disturbing is the number of people who openly admit that the *hejab* is a mere convention or conceit rather than a true act of faith.

The mother of my colleague and translator Akeel started wearing the *hejab* during the sanctions regime. He described her late-life change to the headscarf as "due to her faith" but also as "just what is done now." Ahmed, the dental technician turned fixer, explains the new vogue with a matter-of-factness that obscures the implied violence. "My wife wears the *hejab*. I told her to." He smiles slyly. "But she wears jeans and western clothes." Ahmed is working for several journalists I know, and occasionally I catch rides with them and plumb him for insights. He is Shia, and says he prays regularly but in other ways seems little concerned with Allah and Ali. "If she did not wear a scarf, men on the street might say things to her and then I would have to fight them. It's just better to avoid trouble."

At Baghdad University male followers of Muqtada al-Sadr are known to threaten women who do not dress modestly enough or who violate other Shia moral strictures, like not listening to music during the sacred month of *Muharram*, during which fasting, prayer and self-denial are recommended.[6] Of course, being chaste isn't easy in a society with endemic poverty, a collapsing education system, few career prospects, and a huge population of cash-flush, sexually frustrated foreign soldiers.

The Palestine and Sheraton Hotels, located just off the river, were once quite fancy and catered to oilmen, visiting notables and upscale tourists. Today the high-rise towers and big empty lobbies, lounges and conference rooms are lonely and run-down. Just next door to each other, the hotels form a single armed camp surrounded by tanks, Humvees, barbed wire, blast barriers and sandbagged gun towers. Inside this perimeter live the highly paid TV journalists who broadcast live from that third-story roof deck with the floodlights illuminating the blue-domed mosque just beyond Fardos Square.

The compound also houses businessmen and is frequented by spooks in their undercover spook outfits, as well as the semi-spooks, the private soldiers of Blackwater Security Consulting, the Hart Group, DynCorp International and the other mercenary firms. Fleming summed them up as "those former Special Forces guys who blew out a knee on the last jump." They sit around the lobby in their postmodern colonial Gap wear: light Trek boots, cargo pants, wraparound shades and subdued polo shirts under slim black flak vests. Near to hand are their tricked-out M-4s or expensive Heckler & Koch MP-5 submachine guns.

Lately the Palestine-Sheraton compound has been subject to ever more numerous mortar and rocket attacks. The insurgents launch their assaults from empty lots only a quarter-mile away, in full visibility of other nonmilitarized hotels.

Just outside the compound's wire is the Karada District, a long urbanized peninsula in the Tigris. Across from the hotels toward the river is a stretch of garbage-strewn wasteland, its brown dirt occasionally broken by clumps of trees and dotted with bits of tacky, decrepit sculpture. This was once a park, but now it's a no-man's-land: home to crazy people, trash fires and diseased feral dogs.

On one occasion, when entering the compound from the riverside, several colleagues and I met a large, sickly, molting and vicious mutt just in front of the gate. The beast is sleeping in a mud puddle, but upon our approach it rises from its stinking ditch and moves forward with a deranged growl. Its backside is totally bald and leathery; its mouth, a small window into a wet hell. We keep it at bay by yelling at it and pelting it with rocks. I find the courage to walk past it only when a young African American GI comes to the edge of the wire with the stock of his M-4 against his shoulder, the barrel pointed down but ready to swing up. "It's cool," he says. "I gotcha covered."

"Man! Somebody's gotta whack that mutt," says Fleming, running a big hand over his stubbly scalp. "If the 1st AD wants to help build democracy in Iraq, they should start by wasting that stinking, evil, nasty dog." We all agree: nation building, one dead canine at a time.

In the parking lot of the Sheraton it seems as if the sun is in a rage, strangling the city with heat. The GIs on the tanks all wear black leather gloves: touch the metal without protection and your hands burn and blister. One tank has a bumper sticker on the barrel reading "Question Internal Combustion."

"How hot is it in there?" I ask the soldier on the turret.

"Man, it's, like, 270 degrees."

"Dude, water boils at 240," says Fleming.

"All right, so it's like 150 degrees. I don't know. It's just really fucking hot."

We have come to this hotel fortress from our more anonymous digs for some Turkish coffee and air conditioning and to use the high-speed

Internet café. I am physically drained, soaked in sweat and mentally fried from the heat, the driving, the interviews, and the constant, gnawing, low-level fear. We all drift off in different directions. I am back from checking e-mail, headed for a couch and more coffee when I see that a young woman has joined Akeel in an empty side lounge. Akeel waves me over, and we chat for a bit. The young woman speaks some English. She wears tight blue jeans, has dyed blonde highlights in her curly hair, and says she is here looking for a job. I wander off again but Akeel soon finds me; he's convinced she is a prostitute.

"What makes you think that?"

"I can just tell. You should do an interview with her."

"So let's ask her."

"No, it's better if I ask her, away from you."

After a few minutes, the two of them come back and we relocate to a corner of the Sheraton's musty, catacomb-like hallways and sit on a couch for the interview. She won't give her name but through Akeel's translation she explains the details of her work. For fifteen dollars a session she has sex with American soldiers. She's seventeen, has her own car, and wants to go to college or maybe just leave Iraq. Her father works with the Americans and comes to this hotel on business but has no idea what her work consists of. She says she is not afraid of misery gangs because she has her own car and is careful. Her customers include soldiers; one regular is a captain in the 1st AD.

"Do you use protection with the soldiers?"

She blushes and pauses. "She says she takes the pills," explains Akeel. Does she know about AIDS?

"No condoms?" I ask.

She blushes more deeply and answers directly in English. "Sometimes."

Iraq once had a strong and vibrant working-class movement. In fact, the Baathists were always reacting to that movement with a combination of repression, cooptation and aesthetic and rhetorical imitation. Mohammed's comrades in the Iraqi Union of the Unemployed are trying to resurrect a real workers movement, or a movement of the excluded. In a park across from the so-called Assassins Gate the IUU holds regular demonstrations.

In a way these cadre could be anywhere in the world; they are the same collection of diehards, misfits, self-appointed leaders, and solid, noble regular folks who protest injustice everywhere. Only here they are so outnumbered and the political context so hopeless that it is very hard to willingly suspend disbelief and see the revolution coming—unless it's the one waving a green flag and wearing the black shirts of Muqtada al-Sadr's militia.

The US troops meet the IUU demonstrations with a combination of indifference and repression. At the group's biggest mobilization in the stifling heat of August some fifty of the comrades were arrested by US soldiers and held for a day. One of those detained was Hamid Abdia. He is in a wheelchair and wears a red headband.

"Even though I am in a wheelchair the US soldiers insulted me. But I have the right to a job and to live," says Abdia, the next day back at the site of his arrest. The IUU is on the street again, but their crowds, as far as I can see, rarely reach even a thousand. Ultimately their message of "worker communism" makes little or no sense to the people of Iraq, where workers' symbols were the currency of the old Baathist plutocracy and where Islamist religious rhetoric is now the prevailing discourse of all sides.

As we leave the IWCP's looted bank one day Akeel steps into the street to hail a cab and light a cigarette. He comments: "C.P., Iraqis will never follow these people. I don't know why you're spending so much time with them."

From one of the IUU demos that had finally been broken up by the suffocating heat we move a mile north to explore part of the looted Ministry of Film and Television. Its courtyard is bleached dry, its second-story mosaics look forlorn. On the ground we find a Republican Guard uniform and some old, trampled spools of celluloid: a movie from the seventies showing a family driving through a calmer, Technicolor Baghdad. Then we come across a grenade. Akeel wants to pick it up, claiming that it is somehow inoperable. It sits in a dry blue-tiled fountain. He's reaching for it.

"Hey! I am sure you're right, but please do not pick that up!"

He is dissuaded. Further on is the blasted wreck of an Iraqi tank, and living nearby is Ibrahim Kadum, squatter and father of nine. He explains that he lost his foot in the Iran–Iraq war, and then he lost his home and kebab shop to some of Uday Hussein's boys. Now he squats in these ruins with his wife, nine children, and a shaggy and bleating ewe. He says he loves George Bush. Kadum can't work, so he lives off the meager wages of his children, some of whom do odd jobs in a local market.

Kadum says he was recently told by some of the new Iraqi police that he and all other squatters here must leave these government buildings within a month. Some sixty-five other families from Kadum's old neighborhood also squat in the rubble around him. They all moved here more or less together, though as a network not as an organization. When asked if they will resist the eviction order. Kadum says no.

"Everyone will have to find their own way."

I ask Kadum if he knows about the IUU.

"No. Maybe they can help me."

As we talk a bleary-eyed child approaches with a very realistic-looking plastic pistol and levels it at Fleming's bald head. The gun only shoots plastic pellets.

"Someone's gonna waste that kid if he keeps pointing that at strangers. This is a really fucked-up country," says a rattled Fleming.

Along with the wages of his children Kadum survives on World Food Program donations of flour, legumes, oil, salt, sugar and tea. These allotments are distributed to all 25 million Iraqis, about half of whom depend on the rations for bare subsistence. Yet the scheme, a direct continuation of the oil-for-food program of Saddam's era, was scheduled to end in November 2003. The quick young minds running the Coalition Provisional Authority and within the Halliburton-dominated reconstruction programs had a better idea—they would make room for the magic of the market. From the physical and social rubble of Kadum's home the future of Iraq looks grim, fragmented and desperate.

3

Imperium Delirium

> We dominate the scene and we will continue to impose our
> will on this country.
>
> L. Paul Bremer III, June 29, 2003

A thick plume of black smoke rises from a section of Karrada Street
where US military patrols often stop to buy air conditioners and
DVDs. An American Humvee making just such a stop has parked on a
wide traffic median and been blown to pieces by a remote activated "improvised explosive device," or IED, buried in a dirt planting square. By
total chance my three friends and I are the first press on the scene; behind
us come the two guys from Kent News and Pictures.

Most journalists are busy elsewhere: they have a better story on the
other side of town, where the Jordanian Embassy has been hit with a
massive car bomb, the first of many to follow. The entire international
press corps has been on the perimeter of that mess for about two hours.
We heard the news of the embassy bombing late, and we were finally
headed there when we saw this other column of smoke rising close behind us in our rearview mirror.

"Turn around," Fleming demands. "That's not a trash fire."

We bail out and jog toward the smoke. Karrada Street is empty and totally quiet except for the shopkeepers who huddle in their doorways and
occasionally call out to us in Arabic and English: "Be careful." We move
to the side of the street and creep along past the stores, staying low and
near the cover of the parked cars.

Then we get close enough to see what is going on. About twenty feet
away sit a military transport truck and two Humvees with a handful of
American soldiers crouched behind them. Thirty feet beyond that are the
flaming remains of a third Humvee, blown to smithereens by the massive
IED. Bizarrely, there's no firing, no yelling, no talking, no radio traffic, no
one screaming, but two US soldiers are down. They've been pulled into
one of the vehicles ready for evacuation. So far there are no reinforce-
ments or helicopters overhead. All one can hear is the billowing updraft
of the flame and smoke from the obliterated Humvee.

We crouch and watch, feeling slightly scared and slightly silly: scared
because we can see that this really is war; and silly because we all know
how to act, or think we know how to act, thanks to childhoods full of
war movies.

Then it starts. At first a few loud pops and cracks, then a cacophonous
barrage. It is hard to tell what is happening, but it seems that the ammunition in the burning Humvee is exploding and the troops in the street
are firing and someone in the upper floors of a three-story office mall is
shooting back at them. (Later I meet a CPA-connected aid worker who
was by chance shopping for an air conditioner and got pinned down in a
store just across from the Humvee. He reports that the shooting began
when GIs taking up position in that same shop saw an armed man on a
roof across the street.)

As soon as the storm of lead starts Fleming and I are behind a small
Toyota sedan; I try to merge with the rear wheel to keep as much metal

as possible between me and the madness a few yards away. The shooting subsides. We consider our options.

"Stay here?"

"Go to that shop?"

"This engine block is pretty solid."

"Yeah, and half our bodies are behind rubber tires."

We move to the doorway of a shop. Another round of blasting commences. We hit the ground, pressing our bodies into the dusty concrete.

After a moment it's quiet again. Garrett and Akeel have crossed the street. Fleming and I look at the angle of things and figure it's best to be on the same side of the street as the US troops who have most of the guns and are doing most of the shooting. We cross over, walking quickly but not running, as if the firefight is a big dog that has to be psyched out. The four of us take up position in the doorway of a refrigerator store next to another store selling shoes.

Now armored personnel carriers arrive and disgorge scores of soldiers from the 82nd Airborne. The firing continues, and occasionally we hear a few return rounds. They pass with a sound like hot razors slashing open the air above our heads—*zzzick*. The really close bullets sound like loud cracks.

"That's Kalashnikov, I know the voice," says Akeel. There is a clear bit of national pride in his tone—his countrymen are fighting back—never mind the fact that we are now mixed in with the most forward US troops *and* getting shot at. He and Garrett are cool and collected, rolling video and sound with total equanimity. Fleming and I are a bit less collected: during some of the loudest and most crowded blasts of .50 cals, M-4s, and answering AKs, I lose my nerve completely and duck from the doorway deep into the back of the electronics store. The two shopkeepers are equally freaked out but still very polite. The owner, Ali, offers me water.

We make simple conversation in an improvised pidgin of Arabic, English and fear.

"War, bad. *La, la* war. No fucking good."

"*Nam, la, la* war. *Inshallah salam, salam* Iraq. In Iraq, peace, God willing. *Inshallah.*"

"*Inshallah.*"

The firefight goes on for about two hours, and about halfway through the fight we start moving down toward the targeted building as US troops start moving past us. The whole action is slow and methodical. In many ways it encapsulates the larger dynamics of the war: confusing and labor-intensive, overly and dysfunctionally technological, awkwardly urban. The US troops have far more firepower than they can use, but they don't know exactly where or who the enemy is. There are civilians hiding in every corner, the ground floor of the target building is full of merchants and shoppers, and undisciplined fire will mean scores of dead civilians.

There are the two GIs down. I can't see them, but I am told one has lost his legs and is probably set to die. When a medivac helicopter arrives just overhead, it, too, like much of the military's technology, is foiled. The street is crisscrossed with electrical wires and there is no way the chopper can land to extract the wounded. The soldiers around us look grave and weary.

Eventually some Bradley Fighting Vehicles start pounding the building with mean 25-millimeter shells. Whoever might have been shooting from upstairs is either dead or gone.

The street is now littered with overturned air conditioners, fans and refrigerators, the consumer amulets of progress and domesticity. We've moved up to a point just across from the target building. A store on its ground floor starts burning, and the shopkeeper sobs into Akeel's chest as his life savings go up in smoke. The flames spread to some bushes in front of a house next door. Nearby a cooler of sodas is spilled forlornly on the sidewalk. Further away two civilians lie dead, caught in the cross-fire. A solider peeks out from the hatch of a Bradley and calls over to a journalist.

"Can you grab me one of those Cokes?"

That evening we return to Karrada Street hoping to unpack exactly what had transpired during the attack and the following firefight. But like so much in occupied Iraq, the harder one looks the less one sees.

We find that the burnt-out shop hasn't been totally destroyed, but most of its goods are ruined and miraculously all of the customers and merchants trapped on the ground floor during the firefight are fine. Toward the end of the shooting we had seen them emerge waving their underwear as white flags and then sprint to safety. The fire next door engulfed only the parched bushes in front of the house. The owner of that home and his eight family members had hidden in a small cellar made for just these sorts of occasions.

A crowd of men mill around in front of the scarred office mall. Boys sift through ashes where the Humvee had been; its charred hulk was hauled off earlier by US troops. A kid of about ten holds up the vehicle's tire iron. Two guys, one of them on a bicycle, start shoving each other. The mood of the crowd is both celebratory and a bit angry. The light is orange and fading to dusk.

I interview some witnesses and survivors of the shootout; Garrett wanders into the crowd; Fleming, in a political daze, mutters about how "this is totally fucked up" and disappears into the building's carbonized interior. A boy shows me the undamaged slugs from some burned-out M-4 rounds: clearly debris from the Humvees.

"These are the bullets the Americans shot at me," he says in Arabic, then adds, pointing to the wall: "These are the holes from where the bullets missed me." Akeel tries to suppress an incredulous grin as he translates. Other boys bring shell casings and pieces of the Humvee and request photos. I am interested in reconstructing the insurgency's MO and trying to see how much support it has. But it is getting hard to do interviews. I can't pin down many of the day's details, since everybody keeps chiming in, interrupting each other and offering pieces of the big picture.

"The Americans made this happen. They have destroyed Iraq. There is no economy."

"They force even good Muslims to sell sex movies just to survive."

"Israel is behind all of this. They had made America do these things."

"We all knew this would happen soon. The Americans are ruining everything." And then rather cryptically an old man says: "Many of the young people here are not from Karrada." What did that mean?

"I don't think we should ask about that," says Akeel. It seems to be some sort of resistance reference.

At one level what happened here wasn't anything specific. It was simply the local and momentary iteration of occupation and resistance. "The war" is everywhere like a spectre but only erupts into view for hot moments of chaos, terror and death. With this round of shooting over, the war's larger causes seem to stalk the street, animating the conversation.

A television and radio producer in his mid thirties steps forward. The man has nice clothes, short hair and a neatly trimmed five o'clock shadow—the polished ruffian look preferred by the hip young men of Baghdad. Akeel knows the man from times past, when the producer worked for an English-language pop music and listener call-in station owned by Uday Hussein. Akeel was one of the station's star callers. He lived in Michigan for two years and has a faintly American accent and a vast knowledge of American and British pop culture, so when things were slow the radio station would even call Akeel and put him on the air to offer shoutouts to his peeps and request songs. The station even invited Akeel to a few of its private parties.

The whole scene was a fetishized imitation of some hodgepodge imaginary suburban American youth culture, and broadcast across Baghdad it served not as a cultural fifth column but as an aesthetic buttress to shore up, legitimize and "brand" Saddam, his regime and his crazed playboy sons. In others words, a fascist at war with the US, in the process of transforming his image from that of Arab Nationalist to Political Islamist, used a weird mix of Limp Bizkit, the Red Hot Chili Peppers and Michael Bolton to lull and woo the middle-class youth of his capital. Just one more example of Saddam's bizarrely theatrical flexibility, similar to his donning traditional Kurdish dress during public visits to Kurdistan while simultaneously repressing the Kurds, or praying at Shia mosques while assassinating Shia clerics.

That was long ago and worlds away. Now the producer is livid.

"Where is the electricity? Where is the water? This is the freedom? In 1991 Saddam had the lights back on in two months. Two months! Are you going to tell me the superpower cannot make the lights work? I do not believe it! This is a plan to destroy us and take our oil."

It is a sentiment I begin to hear frequently: "The phones do not work because they do not want us to be able to communicate," says a taxi driver. "Where is the electricity? They are stealing our oil," explains a shopkeeper. One can almost watch the political fallout in real time: every night that the lights blink out or the tap runs dry more Iraqis turn away from America and "the freedom" and reorient toward the resistance, *al-mujahadeen*.

As the radio producer drives home his points an American tank rolls toward us and stops some fifty yards away. Fleming is on top of the building now, snapping photos; a crewman on the tank's turret scans his weapon across roofs. Fleming is snapping in their direction, and the tanker pauses, aims and then passes on without incident. When Fleming descends he's indignant: "Dude drew a fucking bead on me." Two weeks later Mazen Dana, a Reuters cameraman, is killed in almost the same situation, pointing his camera at a tank. We tease Fleming. "Yeah, you should file a written complaint with the war's manager. Gotta get these honkies to stop pointing their guns like that."

A t the center of this sprawling war zone, like the eye of a storm, is a clean, air-conditioned oasis, a land of dreams: welcome to Saddam Hussein's old Palace of the Republic, now the much-storied "Green Zone," the fortress-headquarters of the Coalition Provisional Authority. This huge complex of high modernist architecture, manicured lawns, gardens and palm trees is the spot where L. Paul Bremer III and his army of freshly minted MBAs spend the first year of the occupation fantasizing about a future that will never be.

In these confines bold young ideologues rule the roost, working in splendid isolation on "governance issues" and "privatization." The palace is a blur of pleated khakis, oxford shirts, laptops, backpacks and well-coifed blond hair. As Garrett Scott would later put it, "Iraq is the most important internship of their lives."

The young experts of the CPA live in total fear of the very cities and people they are charged with governing. They are mocked as "occupodians" by their own praetorians—the multicultural, working-class GIs from Fresno, Philly, and the nowhere hamlets of Arkansas who guard the Green Zone palace. Lacking experience with the real Iraq, these postmodern colonialists, the ideological anti-Arabists of the American Empire, spin wildly unhinged plans and dole out vast sums of unaudited, practically unmonitored cash to US contractors. Meanwhile, outside the walls one hears the boom and rumble of IEDs. If the blast goes off at the top or bottom of the hour it is just the military engineers, an Explosive Ordnance Disposal (EOD) squad cleaning up a booby-trap with a controlled blast. If the blast comes at any other time it means something bad.

One early and particularly brilliant occupodian plan was to end food rationing by November 2003. It didn't happen. Among the parties opposing this idea was the US Army, which recognized that such a massive and final pauperization of Iraq's people would have negative effects on "stabilization." Another occupodian plan was to privatize all productive state assets. That scheme bogged down when potential buyers were scared away by threats and escalating violence. Most dramatically, the manager of the state vegetable oil company started firing workers in an effort to streamline the firm, which makes cooking oils, soap and other related products, and prepare it for privatization. Verbal protests and pleas from workers went nowhere, so an unknown gunman followed up these supplications with a bullet to the manager's head. Suddenly, members of the Iraqi Governing Council grew reticent on the issue of privatization.[1]

To my mind the essential character of these carpetbaggers was summed up in the form of Joseph Braude, a multilingual business consultant and author who was hired by the CPA to consult on reconstructing the economy. To his credit Braude did write an informed cultural and historical guidebook to what he imagined would be a pleasant postwar Iraq. Descended on his mother's side from Baghdadi Jews, Braude had never actually been to Baghdad when he wrote his book.

When I interviewed Braude he was cagey about what his contract with the CPA stipulated and how he thought the freedom was progressing in

Iraq. As it turned out, his stint with the CPA was ill-fated and short-lived. After his first short foray to Baghdad, customs officials at Boston's Logan Airport found two priceless Mesopotamian carvings secreted in Braude's luggage. The pieces were estimated to date from 2340–2180 BC and were known to be swag from the Iraqi National Museum because they bore engraved museum ID numbers.

Braude told Customs officials that he knew the items were probably looted from state vaults when he bought them for $200 on the streets of Baghdad.[2] Too bad for the occupodians, since they could have used Braude's talents; he speaks Arabic and clearly understands the nature of the American mission in Iraq.

A t one edge of the CPA's oasis sits the Convention Center. During that first summer of occupation the CPA offered journalists a weird sort of blackmail: every day at three o'clock the Coalition Provisional Authority's spin doctors would address the press in a large air-conditioned auditorium. In Vietnam style we call these confabs "the follies." At first these press conferences happen every day, then only every other day or less frequently.

The ritual begins with a slew of statistics about the "good progress" being made. But the numbers are often mumbled like a Latin mass that no one really understands or cares about; one begins to feel that the driving force is faith, not reason or planning.

"In the last twenty-four hours coalition forces have detained a hundred and forty-nine individuals, conducted over a thousand patrols and twenty raids," says the pale and pudgy Colonel Shields one day. "We have confiscated a hundred and ten diesel-smuggling tanker trucks, and destroyed more than twenty IEDs. Coalition forces completed four civic action projects in the Basra area and ..." On and on it goes until the colonel gets stuck on the word *adjudicated*. "Several of these cases will be ... edjuda-rated, that is, ajew-terated, I mean ..."

Ask Shields how many Iraqis have been killed by US troops and despite his reams of stats he doesn't know. How many women have been raped by misery gangs? No number. How many US soldiers have committed suicide? Any troops busted for looting? Can't say.

Then in the auditorium below a loud snore, followed by snickering laughter from surrounding journalists: the *Los Angeles Times* man, just in from Jordan, is passed out cold. He told me he hadn't napped last night during the dangerous thirteen-hour drive in and obviously the combina-tion of Shields nattering on and the wonderful air conditioning had a powerfully soporific effect. Sharing the GMC in with him was Thomas Friedman, who seems like he can barely keep his eyes open during the numerical incantation. Who can blame him? On the way out of the press conference the *L.A. Times* man tries to play off his nap: "Did the colonel say that fifty or one hundred and fifty oil-smuggling tankers were confis-cated? I missed that bit."

The follies (now greatly scaled back) essentially offer journalists a way to be comfortable and not work, yet feel important and productive. The by-product is that a lot of predigested, spoon-fed pro-Coalition gib-berish gets passed along as news. This equation applies not so much to the full-timers but to the endless slew of quickly rotating staffers from those "mid-sized metro dailies." Tales of press corps incompetence are legion. Michael Birmingham relayed a story of an American journalist who wanted to write about honor killings and misery gangs but couldn't find any rape survivors who would go on record. "It's a Muslim culture. What are these people thinking?" he says over a bowl of oatmeal during one indescribably hot afternoon.

The CPA's Convention Center presents the very essence of disingenuous, obfuscating political dissembling: journalists pretend to ask questions and the occupation's spokespeople pretend to give answers. Back in the day, one of the stars in this circus was Richard Heatly, a goatee-sporting, trilingual New Labour Oxbridge prat who loved to put on the pretense of sparring with the journos. "No doubt, I am sure you will subject me to all manner of cross-examination on this point, but I assure you that the Coalition blah, blah, blah ..." This is of course a form of cryptic flattery that most journalists love, so they play along, offering softball questions like "How well integrated are the international forces into the Coalition's overall plans?"

At somber moments like these, when the fourth estate is busy assiduously serving the sovereign, we raise our hands with difficult questions but rarely seem to get called on. At one Arabic-language-only press conference we score a direct hit: Akeel asks Bremer about soldiers hiring prostitutes. We wanted to know what sort of efforts the military was making to stop the spread of venereal disease to Iraqi women. Bremer didn't like the question and ended the press conference almost immediately. The next day Akeel is a star on the streets of Baghdad: his jab at the boss man had been on Al-Jazeera.

"Why did he run away from you?" asks one shopkeeper facetiously.

"You were so mean to the Americans with those difficult questions," says a cabbie with a wry grin.

When we can't get called on during press conferences Fleming and I inevitably start making each other laugh by scheming up ways to get hold of rubber Saddam Hussein masks, jockstraps and raw chickens so we can start shooting scenes for *Jackass Baghdad,* our version of a popular MTV stunt show with a similar name.

Later in the occupation there surfaces Dan Senor, a robotic GOP operative and former press secretary for Spencer Abraham, the Michigan Republican who became Bush's secretary of the Department of Energy. Getting real information from Senor was like trying to run across a swimming pool full of warm chewing gum. The CPA press office was in fact stacked with former Bush campaign workers, political appointees and former Capitol Hill staffers, by and large a pack of self-deluding zealots.

Below these ranks are other flacks and "helpful" soldiers officially tasked with "facilitating the flow of information." My favorite of these is Sergeant Ingram, a slow-talking, earnest southerner. He never forgets a name and always talks to you as if you're an old friend, but he never gives an inch.

"I'll look into that for you guys… I know we had a group that went down a while ago. I'll see what I can do… Maybe if I rattle their cages a little bit up there we can get some movement on that 'cause I know that time's important to you." But for Ingram time is of no importance whatsoever. He exists in a world where every day is Friday followed by a weekend during which all tasks are either forgotten or taken care of by someone else. "Well, I probably don't need to tell you guys that the gears up there, well, they tend to turn kind of slow…" et cetera, et cetera. Sergeant Ingram could have you waiting forever *and* feeling good about it.

"That man is a *pro*-fessional," says Fleming. "Man, I'd buy a whole swamp from him! I am telling you, don't fuck with Ingram."

Soon we just sum up Ingram's country-talk mind control by quoting the scene from *Star Wars* where Obi-Wan Kenobi (played by Alec Guinness) hypnotizes the Empire's Storm Troopers just by telling them what to think. So when our requests for interviews and a tour of Abu Ghraib prison are again being "worked on" and "looked into," we walk away and tell each other, "These aren't droids you're looking for."

"Nope, they are definitely not," says Fleming. "In fact, I don't even want to see that prison any more. Now all I want is a big, ice-cold Coca-Cola."

Deep in the cool interior of the CPA's compound sits (or sat) the Coalition's hand-picked Interim Governing Council of Iraq, a body of twenty-five notables, many of them former exiles. During its first year the IGC was known mostly for its duplicity, vacillation, inaction, timidity, and interminable deadlock over small and irrelevant decisions. It took the council almost a month just to create a nine-member rotating chairmanship. More concrete tasks—like writing a new constitution, creating government institutions and reviving the economy (or just privatizing everything)—were left to the CPA and later the US Embassy.

The CPA, a policy wonk's Disneyland at the center of hell, rests on a base of brutal and difficult military labor. In that regard the occupation is the product of toiling soldiers who face heat, cold, sand, stench, violence and fear to keep the occupodians and their Iraqi quislings safe and sound inside the bubble.

"No air conditioning out here and forty pounds of body armor. It sucks," says a grunt standing guard at a military complex in Baghdad where Garrett and I have come to deal with some bureaucratic hurdles while trying to set up an embed. I relay to the young grunt how guys like Heatly and Shields say everything is getting better and better every day in every way.

"Don't listen to these guys. We're the working class." I can't believe my ears, but Spc. Peter Zuhan, lately of Linden, New Jersey, was raised in Slovakia, so concepts like "the working class" are not so alien to him, just as they are quite fitting for this situation. "Whatever they tell you," says Zuhan, "it's bullshit. They're camouflaging."

The real function of the CPA (and now the US Embassy) seems to be the intentional mismanagement of reconstruction contracts. The US government's fanatical devotion to firms like Halliburton and Bechtel plus its cultic fixation on "market solutions" like failed privatization efforts have resulted in social and political disaster. By early fall, reconstruction (better understood as the political side of the war) had largely stalled.

The $8 billion to $11 billion spent on reconstruction could have won, or bought, lots of hearts and minds. The political project was simple: co-opt the opposition, construct and buy the loyalty of a puppet government, reconstruct the economy so that average Iraqis had a shovel in hand rather than an RPG. Call it "nation building" or "colonization in the age of ethics" or just call it "looting" and "the freedom" like Akeel does—either way the project of dominating Iraq was bogged down in a morass of corruption from the moment it started. The avarice and graft of the many businesses feeding at the trough of contracts is complemented by the dysfunctional neoliberal hallucinations of the CPA and the Bush team. Their ideological holy grail of market omnipotence, omniscience and beneficence could not be questioned or reevaluated. It seemed that the Bush administration lacked the core of old-school imperialists needed to discipline firms like Halliburton and force them to invest money, subcontract to local businesses and hire Iraqi workers.

To create a functioning colony and prevent the Shia Intifada, the US needed to turn on the lights, provide clean water, give people jobs, impose law and order, and display at least the pretense of respect for Islam and the Iraqi people. This was not an impossible set of tasks, yet the US with Bush and Bremer at the helm headed straight for the rocks.

If one were to follow the best advice of the counterinsurgency experts, like Maj. John Nagl, author of *Counterinsurgency Lessons from Malaya and*

Vietnam: Learning to Eat Soup with a Knife, there would be near total subordination of the "military" side of operations to the "political" side. In other words, the winning of hearts and minds, reconstruction, and job creation would have been considered the central tasks. But on this front the deepest structures of the occupation have always been profoundly flawed, even within the narrow "New American Century" parameters of pure conquest. The occupation suffers from a lack of local knowledge, linguistic isolation, bureaucratic incompetence, Orientalism, arrogance and brutality. But one dynamic above all others has destroyed the American project in Iraq: fraud.

Iraq reconstruction is a racket. The vast majority of the money allocated for tasks such as rebuilding schools, hospitals and utilities has disappeared into the accounts of Bush administration–connected firms like Halliburton and Bechtel. It is worth recalling the back story to all this, since the details are almost unbelievable: Vice President Dick Cheney receives a monthly stipend of $13,000 from Halliburton, a firm he once ran. The US government gives Halliburton roughly $1 billion a month for work in Iraq related to reconstruction and military service contracts. Cheney's legacy to Halliburton was that he bought Dresser Industries for $7.7 billion. Dresser turned out to have billions in outstanding asbestos-related damages to pay.[3] Without the Iraq contracts, Halliburton—which had a net loss of $947 million in the fourth quarter of 2003 despite year-end revenue that was up by 63 percent—would probably be in bankruptcy thanks to the asbestos payments and other problems connected to "creative accounting." That is a mere sliver of the madness.

By mid 2004 the United States had pledged $18.4 billion for reconstruction in Iraq, more than one-third of the $55 billion the World Bank estimates will be necessary to get the country back on its feet. But as investment-banker-turned-journalist Nomi Prins writes, "You wouldn't know that we were dealing with such enormous quantities from the glaring absence of consolidated financial reporting on Capitol Hill. In fact, an endless gush of money keeps streaming out of Washington faster than the White House seems to be keeping track of it." As she found out, no single agency is keeping track of the reconstruction money spent in Iraq, so there is no central accounting mechanism for overseeing the CPA and the contractors. There is no mechanism to determine if money allocated as reconstruction funding even gets spent. A spokesperson for the anti-corruption campaign group Transparency International estimates that 20 percent of reconstruction money has been lost to corruption. Another estimate puts the amount spent on actual rebuilding at about 5 percent of the total outlay, since real oversight is minimal. The CPA's inspector general employs only fifty-eight staff, while the Defense Department manages its Iraq contracts with only twenty-four auditors.[4]

The US taxpayer and the Iraqi public are left to trust the companies involved. But in April 2004 the Associated Press found that ten companies that had previously been fined or convicted due to their corrupt practices had received billions of dollars in Iraq reconstruction contracts. In the lead were Halliburton and Bechtel, which hold the lion's share of the contracts and have paid heavy penalties for overbilling and other shenanigans in the past three years. Another firm in the top ten was given a $780 million contract in Iraq despite convictions for fraud on three federal construction projects and a total ban on receiving US government work. "Together, the 10 companies have paid to resolve 30 alleged violations in the past four years. Six paid penalties more than once. But the companies have been awarded $7 billion in Iraq reconstruction contracts." This was all made possible by the Bush administration when it repealed regulations promulgated by the Clinton administration that had allowed the feds to stop government contracts to firms convicted or penalized in the

previous three years.⁵ Not long after the AP report came this item from
the *Washington Post* of April 28, 2004:

> The US Army has yet to reach a final agreement on price or the exact work to
> be done under nearly $1.8 billion worth of contracts for Iraq reconstruction
> projects that are already underway, a situation that exposes the government
> to cost risks and reduces the chance for savings, according to a draft report by
> the General Accounting Office.
>
> The work encompasses oil fields, the electrical grid, training for the Iraqi
> army and support for the occupying authority, the draft report states. GAO
> auditors also found several instances in which Defense Department contracting
> officers "overstepped" their authority and ordered millions of dollars of no-
> bid reconstruction work that appears unrelated to the contracts…
>
> The draft cites problems with oversight, including on work done as part
> of a $24 million contract in which some experts hired to advise occupying
> authority officials and Iraqi ministries failed to report for duty, did not do the
> work as expected or had stopped working.
>
> The draft concludes that federal agencies "generally complied" with the
> laws and regulations governing no-bid or limited-bid contracts—an issue
> that has drawn congressional attention. But the GAO reviewers do note
> shortcomings in the tasks ordered under various existing contracts.
>
> The GAO review covers nearly $3.7 billion worth of private contracting
> work committed to as of last September—a sliver of the $20 billion that
> Congress has appropriated.⁶

In October 2003, the British charity Christian Aid alleged that $4 billion
in oil revenues that had been banked by the old Iraqi state, seized by the
CPA, and earmarked for reconstruction had simply disappeared into the
"opaque" bank accounts of the CPA and its friends on the Iraqi Interim
Governing Council. When confronted with these charges Bremer simply
waved them away, claiming that all funds were being spent in a "completely transparent" fashion.

In late 2003 when US journalist Pratap Chatterjee went to various reconstruction project sites to compare facts on the ground with what was stated in the bills and inventories, he found that even the few projects allegedly "rebuilt" had barely been touched. His report, published in *Southern Exposure,* showed that key pieces of Iraq's infrastructure—power plants, telephone exchanges, sewage and sanitation systems—had either not been repaired, or had been "fixed" so poorly that they didn't function. One "repaired" school was overflowing with raw sewage; a teacher at the school also reported that "the American contractors took away our Japanese fans and replaced them with Syrian fans that don't work"—and billed the US government for the work. According to Chatterjee, inflated overhead costs, Byzantine subcontracting relationships, and chronically late payment of wages and fees were the name of the game. He estimated that of Halliburton's initial $2.2 billion in contracts only about 10 percent had gone to meeting community needs.[7]

O f course the war is about much more than contracts or even access to oil. Iraq is part of an ongoing project of ever-expanding US power. This vision of a Planet America was laid out quite bluntly in the Bush administration's National Security Strategy document of September 2002, and all three post–Cold War US presidents have in varying forms sought to extend US power as far as possible. Central to these efforts has been prevention of "the rise of a great-power competitor." The two possible candidates for this are an independent European Union or, down the line, China. The now-infamous report from the Project for a New American Century, called "Rebuilding America's Defenses," framed geopolitics in these same terms. Alumni of the PNAC like Richard Perle were key players in shaping George Bush's war plans. (Recall that Secretary of Defense Rumsfeld, also associated with the PNAC, advocated "regime change" in Iraq as early as February 2001.) Thus, if we pull back from the hot streets of Baghdad, zoom out from the immediate situation, it becomes clear that the project of conquering Iraq was from the first tied to a larger strategy of global control.

In his superb book *The Global Gamble: Washington's Faustian Bid for Global Dominance,* Peter Gowan points out that during the Cold War, the other two poles of world capitalism—Europe and Asia (with Japan as its economic engine)—were beholden to the US for protection against Soviet power and regional communist rebellion. After the collapse of communism that set of dependencies dissolved and a new question emerged: How would the US maintain its power over its friends, particularly the developed economies that might become possible "peer competitors"?

In this, oil is key—or rather, American military control and influence over the Persian Gulf and Caspian Basin. Europe imports more than half of its oil, mostly from the Middle East, and the EU's dependence on foreign petroleum is expected to rise to almost 80 percent by 2020 as North Sea reserves run dry. Economies in Asia are even more dependent. In 2002 China got almost 60 percent of its imported oil from the Gulf, and its energy consumption is expected to double or triple in the next two decades. Japan has only five months' worth of reserves, and 88 percent of its oil is imported from the Gulf. India is likewise consuming oil at an accelerating pace. The American economy, on the other hand, only draws about 11 percent of its total consumption from the Middle East. The bulk of US oil imports come from Canada, Mexico and Venezuela.

Thus, conquering Iraq is not about putting more Arab oil into American SUVs so much as it is about positioning US military might as the sole security arbiter upon which all advanced economies are dependent. Permanent US bases in Iraq would greatly enhance this role. Securing the Middle East and its oil reserves would give America important political leverage over the EU and East Asia. (Of course, US petroleum firms would also stand to do quite well and are eager to privatize Iraqi oil and capture potentially huge profits. After all, some of the first laws promulgated by the CPA were those allowing for privatization, foreign ownership and the repatriation of profits. But the oil majors were also very cautious and skeptical about the invasion.)

As energy gendarme, the United States could "dissuade" friends and foes alike from, say, imposing trade tariffs or favoring local firms over US-based multinationals in contracting; it could help open markets to heavily subsidized US agricultural products; it could help line up European and Asian votes when US business and political elites engage in negotiations on topics ranging from environmental regulation and debt relief to the security of Israel. The US as oil gendarme would be able to keep the other core economies in their role of junior partners in the Global North's domination of the Global South. But in the end this grand strategy has turned out to be a pipe dream. There will be no clean victory in Iraq.

Marla Ruzicka is one of the occupation's NGO groupies. She is the type who gets 10 percent of that 10 percent that trickles down to the ground. Known for her dyed blonde hair and flashy style, Marla is talking up the fact that she had leveraged $10 million from the US government so her organization CIVIC can "aid" the victims of US military action. She and CIVIC and the US occupation authorities do not use the term "compensate" because that would imply American culpability. The US government maintains that because Iraq is a war zone, its military is not legally liable when it kills innocents, and so the operative verb is *aid*. I interview Marla at the Hotel Agadeer, a dive favored by Eastern

European journalists and broke American freelancers. It turns out that Marla hasn't actually received $10 million; USAID captured the grant, and the money will not actually be disbursed as aid to the survivors of US military actions but will instead be spent on unspecified development projects that will indirectly "aid" war victims. When I press Marla further it turns out that CIVIC is directly serving only five families who have been "negatively impacted" by US military operations.

Meanwhile, Iraq's hospitals and other public institutions wither. In late April 2004 my colleague Dahr Jamail visited al-Kena Hospital, the country's main facility specializing in rehabilitation services for the disabled and war-maimed. He found that the hospital had "not received an emergency order for prosthetic supplies it filed nine months ago with the US-funded Ministry of Health. Doctors at the hospital, which houses a prosthetics workshop, also complain they are only receiving 5 million Iraqi dinars ($3,500) per month from the Ministry of Health, when the prosthetics workshop alone requires at least 3 million Iraqi dinars ($2,070) per month to properly serve its patients."[8]

In Ramadi I visit a local maternity ward and a children's hospital. Ushered into its bare halls by armed guards, I meet with several young doctors and staff who frankly explain that the hospital has nothing and that they live in fear of the Americans just as they had once feared Saddam. Then Dr. Hamese Hussein, general director of health in Ramadi and Anbar, comes rushing in. He is fluent in English and informs me that he will now answer my questions. Dr. Hussein is officious and frosty but at the same time nervous and suspicious. He examines my press pass slowly and asks several times, "Who are you? What do you want?"

"Do you have enough medicine here?"

"No," he says hesitantly. "The quality is better now, but it is imported and too expensive and we have too little, almost none." Dr. Hussein explains that the Anbar region's whole health care system, which serves Ramadi, Falluja and a dozen major towns, is trying to operate on an $800,000 grant from the CPA. He says he's been running several hospitals and clinics on that cash for almost four months. The money is almost gone, no one is getting paid, and he doesn't know when more money will be disbursed. To buy medicine he has gone to Jordan and made purchases on the open market.

"You only received this cash? No aid groups sent supplies?"

"No. They send us biscuits and cookies, but no medicine. We have supply closets full of cookies."

I had seen several children in Baghdad with enlarged heads and huge veins bulging from their skulls and been told that this condition and other bizarre cancers and childhood diseases are linked to roughly 1,700 tons of depleted uranium–tipped weaponry that the United States used on Iraq during both wars. The NGO Child Victims of War says that "the number of Iraqi babies born with serious deformities has risen from 3.04 per thousand in 1991 to 22.19 per thousand in 2001. Babies born with Down Syndrome have increased nearly fivefold and there [has been] a rash of cases of previously little-known eye problems."[9]

I ask Dr. Hussein if he sees many children with symptoms related to possible radiation poisoning. The director says nothing; his staff of neatly dressed skinny young men stand awkwardly around the office.

"This is an important issue. The world needs to know about these things. Do you see children who suffer from radiation sickness or not? It's a simple question."

"I cannot answer."

"What do you mean? Why not?"

Another long pause. Dr. Hussein's tough composure softens and he offers something of a coded apology: "This is the freedom."

4

With the Grunts

Human beings become pawns, manipulated and moved
around like chess pieces. Those struggling to survive in a morally bankrupt universe find that there are few restraints left.

Chris Hedges, *War Is a Force That Gives Us Meaning*

An M-16 rifle hangs by a cramped military cot. On the wall above
is a message scrawled in thick black ink: "Ali Babba, you owe me a
strawberry milk."

It's a private joke, but could easily summarize the worldview of many
American soldiers here in Baghdad, the fetid basement of Donald Rumsfeld's house of victory. Trapped in the polluted heat, often poorly supplied
and cut off from regular news, many soldiers find themselves fighting a
guerrilla war that they neither wanted nor trained for, nor fully believe in
or understand. Here, the high-tech weaponry that so emboldens Pentagon bureaucrats is largely useless, and the grinding work of counterinsurgency is done the old-fashioned way—by hand. On the urban battlefields
of central Iraq, "shock and awe" and all the other "new-way-of-war"
buzzwords are drowned out by the din of diesel-powered generators, Islamic calls to prayer and the occasional pop of small arms fire.

It is noon and the mercury hangs at 115 Fahrenheit. Garrett and I are "embedded" with Alpha Company of the 3rd Battalion of the 124th Infantry, a National Guard unit made up mostly of college students from north Florida.

The commanding officer, Captain Rodney Sanchez, assigned us to 2nd Squad, 3rd Platoon, led by Staff Sergeant Kreed Howell. "Best and the brightest," says the executive officer, Captain McClain, as he leads us to meet Sergeant Howell. It's the dog days of August in Iraq and the heat is so intense as to be otherworldly; it almost passes hot into some other state. The ensuing risk of dehydration and disorientation means that Alpha Company has to limit patrols to three or four hours a day. So most of our time with Howell's squad is relatively uneventful, spent hiding out from the heat, lying low and talking.

At age thirty-one Kreed Howell is a bit older than most of the other eight men in his squad. Muscular and clean-cut, he was never in the regular military. "Straight Guard," he says. He comes across as a relaxed and natural leader with the gracious bearing of a proper southern upbringing. Most of the guys here are white, but there is a sizable minority of Black and Latino soldiers as well. Many have done time in the regular army, often with elite groups like the 82nd and 101st Airborne, and roughly 65 percent of these soldiers are or were in the public university system, most of them at Tallahassee State.

They've traded six years with the Guard for free tuition. There's also a smattering of poor country boys who didn't go to college or couldn't get into the army, or wanted to be soldiers but didn't want to leave home. Typically, time in the Florida Guard means occasional weekends in the Pine Barrens or directing traffic during hurricanes. These guys got sent to Iraq.

Mobilized in December 2002, this battalion crossed over from Kuwait on Day One of the invasion. Serving in the war by guarding Patriot missile batteries just behind the front lines, they saw lots of grim things but not much action. Now they are stationed in Baghdad, bivouacked in the looted remains of a Republican Guard officers' club, a modernist slab of polished marble and tinted glass that the GIs have fortified with plywood, sandbags and razor wire. Surrounding the base is a chaotic working-class neighborhood of square two- and three-story sand-colored homes and apartment buildings; not far away is the muddy Tigris River. Just to the north is Adhamiya, one of Baghdad's most restive and tenaciously Baathist areas. Alpha Company's mission is to police this neighborhood in a manner called "peace enforcement." In other words, there is no peace to "keep" and no clear enemy to fight: the mission is urban counterinsurgency with all the brutality and frustration that implies.

Since they got here, the guardsmen have been conducting regular raids and receiving low-level attacks with RPGs and small arms. Two guys from Alpha Company were shot; one lost a lung. A few "Hajis"—GI slang for Iraqis—have been shot, and many more arrested. But there seems to be no end in sight: for every "bad guy" busted there are always two more punks rolling by with grenade launchers, or another IED discovered in a heap of trash. The work of pacification is taking on a deadly, dehumanizing and work-a-day quality. The longer they stay here, the more hardened these soldiers become.

At first the 3rd of the 124th was supposed to be in Baghdad for only three months. Then it became five months, then seven, and eventually it would be a whole year. Each time the unit's deployment is extended, the orders come at the last minute as if specially designed to demoralize the soldiers and dash the hopes of their families.

Behind the sleek but somewhat battered tinted glass box that is the old officers' club is a three-story dormitory, a warren of small one-bedroom apartments, each holding a nine-man squad of soldiers and all their gear. This is where we spend most of our time. One side of the dorm has an open-air stairway and terraces lined with black marble looking out onto an apartment building housing Iraqi civilians. Off these open walkways are the rooms into which are packed about 150 guys. Their sweaty fatigues drape the banisters while inside the cramped dark rooms the floors are covered with cots, heaps of flak vests, guns and, where possible, big water-based Iraqi air conditioners called swamp coolers.

In one room a guy plays guitar while around him sit a group of glum grunts, stripped down to black shorts and gray t-shirts emblazoned with "Army." On a cot nearby another kid wears big headphones and watches a war flick on a laptop. The walls are inscribed with carefully lettered graffiti—poems, slogans and bizarre jokes. On the ground floor is the company's makeshift little exercise room where the "Joes" have built a chinning bar and a bench press and have some crude metal weights. A message on the wall reads: "Pain is temporary. Glory is forever."

"This is nice to have weights," I say to Sergeant Golder, a huge blond, pale-eyed NCO who is connected to the command post but hangs out and lifts with Howell.

"We bought them from some locals," he says between sets. "But like everything else in this country, they're stolen."

Up in the two-room suite where Howell's squad lives, Sergeant Jayce Sellers is lounging on his cot. "We're getting just a little bit stir crazy," explains the lanky Sellers. "We've watched every one of our movies like a hundred times. I've seen every one of our porn flicks so many times I know every freckle on every ass. I don't even need to watch them any more, I just rerun the scenes in my head." His demeanor is typical of this squad, friendly but serious with a wry and angry sense of humor. On the side of his helmet Sellers has, in violation of regs, attached the unmistakable pin and ring of a hand grenade. Next to it is written "Pull Here." One gets the impression that if there were ever to be a mutiny among these troops Sellers would be the guy to kick it off.

Back on "Planet Earth" Sellers is a sign painter in Port St. Joe, a small beach town on the "Forgotten Coast" of Florida's panhandle. Before college and the Guard he was in the military as a tanker with the 3rd Armored Cavalry Regiment. The 3rd ACR is also in these parts—they spent much of the first year of occupation wreaking havoc all over the Sunni Triangle.

At twenty-nine, Sellers is more self-reflective and open than most of the younger soldiers. Leaning back on his cot, he is drawing a large intricate pattern on a female mannequin leg. The wall above him displays a photo collage of pictures retrieved from a looted Iraqi women's college. Smiling young ladies wearing the *hejab* sip sodas and stroll past buses. They seem to be on some sort of field trip. Nearby are photos clipped from *Maxim* of coy young American girls offering up their pert round bottoms. Dominating it all is a large hand-drawn dragon—"That's in honor of an ex-girlfriend, total bitch"—and a photo of Jessica Lynch with a bubble caption reading: "Hi, I am a war hero. And I think that weapons maintenance is totally unimportant."

The boys don't like Jessica Lynch and find the story of her rescue ridiculous. Most of the soldiers I met in Iraq didn't like Lynch: they felt that her story was all hype and blamed her rather than the Pentagon spin doctors who concocted the tale. The frequent anti-Jessica comments also carry a gendered subtext: girls shouldn't be crashing our macho fantasies here in Iraq. Howell's squad had been down the same road a day before Lynch's unit was ambushed and they are entirely unsympathetic.

"We just feel that it's unfair and kind of distorted the way the whole Jessica, quote rescue, thing got hyped," explains Howell.

"In other words, you'd have to be *really* fucking dumb to get lost on that road," chimes in the less diplomatic Spc. John Crawford.

"I wasn't gonna be that blunt," says Howell with a smile. Howell has the type of hospitable but stressed-out demeanor that one sees in other men of his age and rank: staff sergeants, responsible for eight guys' lives, old enough to handle the job but still young and inexperienced enough to be deeply freaked out by the responsibility.

Just off the squad's main room is a small windowless supply closet loaded with packs and gear. There's just enough extra room in the closet for a chair and a little shelf on which sits a laptop. Crawford is at the computer. Hanging by this tiny desk is a handwritten sign from "the management" requesting that soldiers masturbating in the supply closet "remove their donations in a receptacle." Instead of watching porno DVDs, Crawford is here to finish a short story.

"Trying to start writing again," he says wearily. Crawford is a fan of Tim O'Brien, particularly *The Things They Carried*. He shows me his short story, which is about a vet who is back home in north Florida trying to deal with the memory of having mistakenly blown away a child while serving in Iraq. The story is fiction. Crawford is three credits short of a BA in anthropology and wants to go to graduate school. Howell, a Republican, amicably describes Crawford as the squad's house liberal. Crawford's not sure that he is a liberal—he just thinks that the war is about global conquest, not WMDs or terrorism.

"We're a pretty Republican squad," says Howell. "Is *The Nation* a Republican magazine?"

Along with Howell, Sellers and Crawford the squad includes several other large personalities. Sergeant Tyler Brunelle, like Sellers, is a team leader. He's tall and skinny, confident and talkative. Brunelle, it turns out, did not have to deploy because he was in a special training program. But his college roommate and some close friends were all in his company. If they were going, so was he. So he volunteered, for his friends.

Brunelle's closest buddy is John Whigham, whose body can't process the abundant calcium in the Baghdad water, so he carries kidney stones ranging from five to nine millimeters, and he can't get home for treatment. Frederic Pearson, aka Diddy, is the only African American in the squad. At home he is a court clerk and hopes to go to law school. "All the Hajis think he's Sudanese," says Brunelle.

"I tell 'em, 'Nope, it's Panama City, man. Panama City.'"

T. J. Hightower is sweet and retiring, short with glasses, an unlikely soldier. "Guy's a Haji magnet," says Howell. "They just love him." Hightower is so relaxed, or maybe just lax, that he is known to remove the heavy ceramic plates from his flak vest when heading out on patrol. Then there's Spc. Omar Ortega from Peru; he's another very unlikely soldier, short, boyish, bespectacled, almost pudgy. Ortega seems depressed and very shy.

As we prepare for our first patrol Howell and Brunelle say they are confident that the military can keep a lid on Iraq and eventually mop up the resistance. But it's not always the "Joes" who have the upper hand; increasingly "Haji" is setting the agenda. Not long before, Garrett and I had spent the afternoon pinned down on Karrada Street inside that cacophonous, furious gunfight. After that shootout, while sucking down beers in our hotel room and watching the strange offerings of Libyan state TV piped in by satellite, we promised ourselves we'd stay out of Humvees and away from US soldiers. But that was yesterday, or the day before. Now John Crawford is helping us get into some borrowed body armor, and soon we are headed out on patrol.

The heat is stifling. It seems that time itself creeps under the weight of it. As we move out with the nine soldiers the mood is somewhere between tense and bored. Crawford, gum-chewing and cocky, in narrow wraparound sunglasses, carries the squad automatic weapon, or SAW, a huge bipod M-249 machine gun that shoots 750 rounds a minute. The official name seems deliberately ironic. As we leave the gate Crawford mockingly introduces himself to no one in particular: "John Crawford. I work in population reduction."

"Watch the garbage. If you see wires coming out of a pile, it's an IED," warns Howell. It's a bizarre scene: a military patrol walking through a crowded city full of civilians and cars. It doesn't seem like war, but that's the way Iraq is most of the time. We walk fast through back streets and rubbish-strewn lots, pouring sweat in the late afternoon heat. Local residents watch the squad with a mixture of civility, indifference and open hostility. On one narrow street some children crowd around.

"We're pretty safe if there are kids around 'cause Haji usually won't kill kids just to get at us," says Howell.

"Yeah, Haji doesn't kill kids unless, you know, he's just in the mood to kill kids," says Crawford, still smacking his gum and scanning the scene from behind his shades, the heavy SAW strung along his waist.

"Sometimes we sham," explains Howell. "We'll just go out and kick it behind some wall. Watch what's going on but skip the walking. And sometimes at night we get sneaky-deaky. Creep up on Haji, so he knows we're all around." We walk along this way and that, up one street, down another. An Iraqi man shouts, "When? When? When go?!" The soldiers ignore him.

"I am just walking to be walking," says the laconic Diddy. "I just keep an eye on the rooftops, look around, and walk."

We move up and down more streets, then loop through a derelict lot dotted with palm trees and piles of garbage and ash. The squad is looking for IEDs. Sellers kicks an empty paint can and knocks through the heaps of trash with his boots. More walking and then we stop at a gas station to check for people illegally selling gasoline from jerry cans. Then more fast walking, weaving through the streets and traffic, down to the river to another lot.

Three months from now one of the guys in Alpha Company, a twenty-year-old kid named Alan Wise, will be killed by an IED at the edge of this lot. The blast will send metal up under Wise's helmet and through the side of his head, spilling his brains into his helmet and down onto his flak vest. Howell's squad will have to bring his body in and clean the gore off his gear.

But today there is no IED, only some men drinking and selling beer. The squad stops a few cars and searches for contraband, and convinces one plastered motorist to let a friend drive him home. "Hey, I drink beer, too, man. But you're drunk," says Howell affably. Then it's back to "the Club" to rest before another patrol.

Inside the wire and back in the relative safety of the base, the soldiers strip down to loose black shorts and lounge around in the heat trying to rehydrate. The 124th is on a water ration: only two liters of bottled water a day. After that the Joes are forced to drink from the "water buffalo," a portable chlorination tank on wheels that turns the amoeba-infested dreck from the local taps into something like hot swimming-pool water. Mix this with bright orange or green powdered Gatorade and you can wash down the famously bad MREs (Meals Ready to Eat).

The water ration is just one way in which the military treats these soldiers like unwanted stepchildren. Among the American troops in Iraq there is a two-tiered system. First class is for the regular military; Reservists and the National Guard populate second class. During the first full year of occupation about 40,000 of the total US troop strength of 130,000 are these citizen-soldiers, the neo-draftees. These men and women (there is a surprising number of women soldiers serving in dangerous jobs in Iraq) tend to be older and better educated than the regular army but very poorly treated.

This unit's rifles are retooled hand-me-down M-16s from the Vietnam War; most regular army units have upgraded to a similar but improved weapon called the M-4. They have inadequate radio gear, so they buy their own, unencrypted, Motorola walkie-talkies. The same goes for flashlights, knives, and some components for night-vision sights. The low-performance Iraqi air conditioners and fans, as well as the one satellite phone and payment cards shared by the whole company for calling home, were also purchased out of pocket from civilian suppliers. (A study found that one in four dead GIs was killed because the military didn't provide properly armored vehicles or adequate body armor.)

To top it all off the guardsmen must endure the pathologically uptight culture of the army hierarchy. The 3rd of the 124th is now attached to the newly arrived 1st Armored Division, and when it is time to raid suspected resistance cells it's the seasoned guardsmen who have to kick in the doors and clear the apartments.

"The 1st AD wants us to catch bullets for them, but won't give us enough water, don't let us wear 'do rags, makes us to roll down our shirtsleeves so we look proper! Can you believe that shit?" Sergeant Sellers is pissed off.

The soldiers' improvisation extends to food as well. After a month or so of occupying the Club, Captain Sanchez allowed two Iraqi entrepreneurs to open shop on his side of the wire; one runs a slow-speed Internet café, the other a kebab stand where the "Joes" pay US dollars for grilled lamb on flatbread.

"The Haji stand is one of the only things we have to look forward to, but the 1st AD keeps getting scared and shutting it down." Sellers is on a roll, and he's not alone. Even the lighthearted Howell, who insists that the squad has it better than most troops, chimes in.

"The one thing I will say is that we have been here *entirely* too long. If I am not home by Christmas my business *will* fail." Back in Panama City, Howell is a building contractor; he has a wife, a baby, equipment, debts and employees.

Perhaps the most shocking bit of military incompetence is the unit's lack of formal training in what's called "close-quarter combat." The urbanized mayhem of Mogadishu may loom larger in the discourse of the military's academic journals like *Parameters* and the *Naval War College Review,* but many US infantrymen, including this unit, are trained only in large-scale open-country maneuvers—how to defend Germany from a wave of Russian tanks. Since "the end of the war" these guys have had to retrain themselves in the dark arts of urban warfare.

"The houses here are small, too," says Brunelle. "Once you're inside you can barely get your rifle up. You got women screaming, people and furniture everywhere. It's insane."

The stories that flow from these men are alternately funny, sick and sad. There's Howell's failed attempt to shoot a dog— he missed despite being "sniper qualified." For months afterward guys occasionally address him as "Sergeant How-*woow-woow*-well."

There's the story of Howell's succession to staff sergeant after the squad's old leader, Sergeant Garcia, got busted looting stockpiled cash from a suspected resistance operative. A local informant had passed a tip to Garcia while he was guarding the gate. The informant said a leader of the Fedayeen (Saddam's old paramilitary special forces) was holed up near the Club with huge sums of cash and some guns. Instead of handing this bit of intelligence north, up to CO Sanchez and the intel folks, Garcia got the bright idea of launching his own secret raid. He gathered half of his squad and half of another squad and without permission slipped out the back gate of the Club.

Brunelle was one of the soldiers that Garcia brought on the maneuver. Hunched on the edge of his cot Brunelle recalls the shambolicly unorthodox heist-raid: "We hit the door and this guy's in there with only his family. He doesn't try to resist. We look around and find this suitcase full of twenty-dollar bills, maybe twenty thousand dollars. But then we got into this closet and found these, like, laundry bags full of millions and millions of dinars and more dollars. That's when I was like, what the fuck is going on, we've got to report this. But fucking Garcia tries to get all slick and keeps some of the money and some guns and walkie-talkies." Brunelle shakes his head and takes a swig of bright green sugar water.

Eventually the CIA got involved and the squad was sent to CPA headquarters in the Green Zone. The Fedayeen man was "flipped," turned into an informant.

"I guess the CIA gave him a sat' phone and said, 'You work for us now,' and then turned him back out to the street," says Brunelle. Once he was free the Fedayeen operative asked the CIA for his stolen money, pistol and walkie-talkies back. "Fucking Garcia gave one of the 'terps [interpreters] one of the dude's pistols." So Garcia was busted down a rank and moved to another squad, Howell was promoted, and the whole thing was more or less papered over.

"Nobody fucking liked Garcia, anyway," says Crawford.

Surprisingly, there seem to be fewer sexual shenanigans between US troops and Iraqis than one might imagine. This is due in part to the lack of safe rear areas: the situation in Baghdad and other urban centers is simply too dangerous, and the local interpretation of Islam militates harshly against such exchanges. In Iraq the cities are the front lines: there is no R-and-R among the bright lights of Baghdad.

But when I ask about the sex trade one story surfaces about four soldiers who "tag-teamed" a seventeen-year-old prostitute in an empty room near the Club's back gate, away from the eyes of the CO. It's a story like so many that reflects in specific form the general tendency of imperial warfare to corrupt then liberate the appetites of soldiers, administrators and even journalists.

It started when a young woman came to the back gate and offered sex for twenty bucks per man. "Ficky-fick?" she asked, using the Iraqi slang for sex. As one of the guys put it, "I was like, damn, I could die tonight. This could be the last time I ever have sex." And so the young men, far from home, desperate for release, armed and allowed to tear apart people's homes, put guns to strangers' heads, and arrest, detain and threaten anyone they see fit, did the obvious and took the young prostitute up on her offer.

"She really earned her pay that day."

Eventually the talk turns to the CO, Rodney Sanchez. I immediately liked Sanchez when I met him, but I soon learned that his men almost uniformly loathed him. The CO's sins began with his first address to the troops upon taking command of the company a few months before the war. As one soldier explained it, Sanchez committed the ultimate military faux pas by immediately bragging about his background in the active-duty National Guard Special Forces. At the first company address he allegedly dipped his shoulder and crassly pointed out his "long tab," the patch reading "Special Forces."

"You just don't do that shit," says Brunelle, himself a former Army

Ranger. Like a lot of the young men in Alpha Company his father served in the military—Vietnam—and saw lots of combat. Brunelle and Crawford, both from military families, have absorbed that ethos of macho modesty: respect is earned; decorations and qualifications are not pointed out or bragged about.

The CO's next mistake was to get most of his company wiped out in a war game exercise. "We started taking fire, and he didn't wait for the PL [platoon leader] to report, he just sent us running through the woods and we all got wasted," explains a soldier. Sanchez's final sin was committed during another botched war game, when he called in a fake artillery strike on his own forward observers.

"In the regular army you'd get canned for that sort of thing," the guy comments. As a warm-up for the invasion of Iraq it did not bode well. Then in Iraq, Sanchez did things like micro-manage ambushes and screw them up. Howell's squad was once sent out to catch a crew of insurgents who were planning to hit the Club with RPGs, but Sanchez refused to give the squad permission to fire on the carload of attackers, even as the vehicle circled the building several times. In the end the insurgents managed to hit the Club with an RPG. Sanchez of course blamed Howell, even though the CO had prevented the squad from firing on the attackers when the chance presented itself.

On another occasion the CO ordered Howell and Brunelle to sweep an area on foot where there was a known IED. By the time Alpha Company was garrisoned in Baghdad the soldiers under Sanchez by and large thought of him as an inept and arrogant amateur.

"It's not just the traditional thing of the grunts hating the officers—this guy really sucks," says Sellers.

A common theme in soldier talk is the gore and horror of war. Lots of grunts trade digital photos of Iraqi corpses and the lumps of burnt flesh that are sometimes the only remains. Sellers and Brunelle matter-of-factly show us a few digital mementos of a recent encounter.

"These guys shot at some of us, so some of our guys lit 'em up, put two fifty-cal rounds in their vehicle. One went through this dude's head and into the other guy's hip," explains Brunelle. The third man in the car lived. "His buddy was crying like a baby. Just sitting there bawling with his friend's brains and skull fragments all over his face. One of our guys came up to him and is like, 'Hey! No crying in baseball!'"

"I know that stuff probably sounds sick," says Sellers, "but humor is the only way you can deal with this shit." And just below the humor is volcanic rage. Someone mentions how he recently "kicked the shit out of a twelve-year-old kid" who menaced him with a toy gun.

There's the story of a friendly-fire incident in which a guardsman shot an armed Iraqi during a house raid, only to be shot by his own sergeant entering through the back of the house. Later on comes the story of a soldier in Bravo Company who has children back home and mistakenly blew the head off a little girl in Baghdad. To pick at the psychological wounds, and maybe to banish their own demons and sorrows, some of the guys get on the radio net and start provoking the father/soldier with anonymous necrophilic jibes: "Man, what's wrong with you? We would've given you twenty bucks if you'd brought her corpse over here while she was still warm."

These young guys from rural and suburban Florida feign a callous disregard for the world, but it is clear that the war is eating at them. They are proud to be soldiers and don't want to come across like whiners, but they are furious about what they've been through. They hate having their lives disrupted and put at risk. They hate the military, or at least the Guard, for its stupidity, its blowhard brass living comfortably in Saddam's palaces, its feckless lieutenants who do stuff like raid the wrong house despite clear directions and worried suggestions from the grunts to consult the intelligence. They hate Iraqis for trying to kill them. They hate the country for its dust, heat and sewage-clogged streets. They hate having killed people. And because they are, in the main, just regular, well-intentioned guys, one senses the distinct fear that someday some of them may hate themselves for what they have been forced to do here.

To assuage these pressures many turn to pharmaceuticals. In the big city of Baghdad, "the freedom" means cheap drugs. No law and order means no need for prescriptions, so Baghdad is awash in high-quality steroids, painkillers and sedatives. Military squads will stop on patrol and take on supplies from the local pharmacy. A lot of soldiers, in Alpha Company and elsewhere, are "juicing" on steroids, taking a subcutaneous shot in the butt once every week. It's the drug that makes you stronger, mean and angry. How could the army object? And to calm those same 'roid-hyped emotions, there is always plenty of cheap Iranian Valium to help you get a solid night's sleep after patrol.

Among the regular Valiumheads I met in Baghdad were journalists, NGO workers, alcoholics from devout Moslem families hoping to hide their abuse, hotel staff, and an upright young college girl whose father and brother were lost somewhere in Abu Ghraib prison. People talk about it openly, just like they talk about IEDs. "Yeah, I know it's all very stressful. Have you discovered Valium?" At times it seems like the whole city is high, floating in a diazepam haze, coasting through one deranged situation after another with pharmaceutically enhanced ease. War and the risk of being killed give one license to do all sorts of self-destructive things.

On our last time out with Howell's squad we roll at night in two Humvees. Now there's more evident hostility from the young Iraqi men loitering in the dark. Most of these infantry soldiers don't like being stuck in vehicles. "We're legs, infantry. I hate these Humvees," says Howell while scanning the rooftops and doorways with occasional blasts from a floodlight. At the sight of a particularly large group of youths clustered on a blacked-out corner the Humvees stop and Howell bails out into the crowd. There is no interpreter along tonight.

"Hey, guys! What's up? How y'all doing? OK? Everything OK? All right?" asks Howell in his jaunty, laid-back north Florida accent. The sullen young men fade away into the gloom, except for two who shake the sergeant's hand. Howell's attempt to take the high road, winning hearts and minds, doesn't seem to be for show. He really believes in this war. But in the hot Baghdad night his efforts seem tragically doomed.

Watching Howell I think about the civilian technocrats working with L. Paul Bremer III at the Coalition Provisional Authority. I recall a group of them drinking and laughing poolside at the cushy Al-Hamra Hotel (they cycle in on three-month contracts). The electricity is out half the time, most people are unemployed, and the occupodians hold endless meetings about nothing. Meanwhile, the city seethes. The Pentagon, likewise, seems to have no clear plan; its troops are stretched thin, lied to, and mistreated. The whole charade feels increasingly patched together, poorly improvised. Ultimately, there is very little that Howell and his squad can do about any of this. After all, it's not their war. They just work here.

5

Meeting the Resistance

People say to me, "You are not Vietnamese. You have no jungles and swamps to hide in." I reply "Let our cities be our swamps and our buildings be our jungles."

Tariq Aziz, Iraq's Deputy Prime Minister,
April 7, 2003

Adhamiya is resistance country. The graffiti in this heavily Baathist and Sunni neighborhood strike a defiant posture: "Saddam, in our souls and with our lives we will sacrifice for you." Or, "God protect and guide the hand of *al-mujahadeen.*" The US military considers Adhamiya one of Baghdad's most dangerous sectors; American patrols are regularly attacked here, and when the Shia rose up in April 2004 this was one of the first Sunni strongholds to express solidarity with al-Sadr's Mahdi Army.

The neighborhood's focal point and political center is the Abu Hanifa Mosque and its surrounding walled sanctuary, which sits at the tip of a wide peninsula formed by a bend in the Tigris. Spreading out to the east from Abu Hanifa is a shopping district and the Adhamiya souk. Its streets are old, tight and dirty with rotting food, flies and muck. Its tiny shops sell everything from inexpensive silver and cloth to vegetables and fresh greasy strips of raw lamb, kebabs and strong tea. Abu Hanifa is the last place Saddam was seen before going underground. And it was in this same spot that two *Time* journalists were badly wounded by a grenade assault. The blast sprayed the famous war photographer James Nachtwey with shrapnel, lacerating his hands, abdomen, groin, legs and shins. His colleague Michael Weisskopf lost his right hand when he pitched the grenade out of the Humvee in which it had landed. When Saddam was captured three days later, the neighborhood's streets exploded in spontaneous protest. Masked resistance fighters emerged holding grenades and Kalashnikovs and the protests ended in nighttime clashes with US troops.

Howell and the Florida National Guardsmen of the 3rd of the 124th patrolled the area just south of Adhamiya. When they finally left in January 2004, Alpha Company had lost one KIA and taken seven wounded. The troops stationed just north of them, in Adhamiya proper, had numerous killed and maimed.

The mostly Sunni people of Adhamiya count among themselves many former civil servants, mid-level government functionaries, Baath Party members, military officers and intelligence operatives. These people actually *love* Saddam. When you ask what they think of the deposed and humiliated dictator, the answer is always the same. "He is our president." "Life was better under Saddam." "I love him." "He is a strong man." "He helped Iraq." Dig further, and it turns out that more than a few of these same people have a family member who was in some way abused by the old regime: a brother jailed for avoiding military service or press-ganged into the Fedayeen; a father forced into the Baath Party or shaken down in some protection racket masquerading as Baathist activism; a sibling killed in one of Saddam's ill-advised wars. But now all that is forgotten. Such is the cultural imprint of a totalitarian society: there is no history, only useful rhetoric, the endless present in which the powerful continually rewrite the past. And now in Sunni Iraq many people genuinely love Saddam for the sovereignty, better times and power he symbolizes. More practically, they love the resistance.

Akeel knows people in Adhamiya. He lived there for a while, and when I tell him I want to meet the resistance, he is at first concerned—an emotion he reveals with an uncharacteristic blank stoicism. Then he gets excited. "OK, C.P. We'll see. We'll go up there and talk to some people."

Akeel is in his element when the job is dangerous. He was in the Iraqi army and forced to train with an elite unit but was relieved of duty after an injury. As my colleague and interpreter he gets bored and strains to stay focused during interviews about humdrum subjects such as broken electrical systems or empty hospital shelves. But if the job is to plunge into the hostile unknown, to drive fast toward the loud noise, or show up unannounced at some whacked-out Sunni mosque in the boondocks, he is as nimble as a cat: full of smiles, jokes, crazy stories, always ready for more cigarettes, more tea. And when necessary he is somber, sad, deeply moved, knowing when not to translate until later just to make a host feel safe. The performance, which is both very genuine and classic journalistic guile, usually puts people at ease.

During the first year of occupation, Iraq's Sunni-dominated armed underground had almost no overt political presence; there was no force to play Sinn Féin to the underground's IRA. The Shura council, a body of Sunni clerics and religious parties formed in January 2004, appeared to be taking on this role. But the closest thing to an Iraqi Sinn Féin are the mosques, and they are less a force than a collection of forces, a world marked by countless competing personalities and doctrines. (Unlike the Shia, the Sunni have no clear ecclesiastical hierarchy.) Other than scattered flyers and occasionally issued communiqués taking credit for attacks or threatening "traitors" and collaborators, the guerrillas speak to the world only with their IEDs and RPGs.[1]

Despite its secrecy, the basic contours of the resistance seem clear. There are distinct but overlapping networks of groups, organized into autonomous cells. The most common type of resistance cell seems to be Baathist and made up of former military or intelligence veterans, many of whom are also deeply religious and work with the communities in their mosques. These are "former regime elements," as the Coalition spokesmen like to call them, but they are not necessarily Rumsfeld's "dead enders," hopeless Saddamists fighting for a restoration of the "hero leader."

After all, Iraq was always more than just one man. Saddam's security forces always contained factions, interest groups, bureaucratic officialdoms that were self-serving and semi-autonomous. These forces still exist, or pieces of them do, as a networked nationalist underground with an Islamic, though not fundamentalist, worldview. It is worth pointing out that Saddam's regime was secular in that its laws were mostly not based on religion. But in this case *secular* did not mean the absence of religion. Rather it meant a pluralism of faiths: the motifs of Islam always figured prominently in the state's trappings, but some of Saddam's closest advisers were Christian or Sufi.

The resistance also includes non-Baathists, nationalists organized along lines of religion and clan. But even these forces usually interface with components of the fallen regime's more than 400,000-strong security forces. And beginning in the winter and bursting into full recrudescence during the spring of 2004 were the Shiite militiamen of al-Sadr's Mahdi Army, or Jeshi Mahdi, who formed another enemy of America. As the crisis grew, many mainstream Shiites joined the Mahdi in their fight, if not in their religious beliefs.

There is also speculation that some renegade elements of the Badr

Brigades—the 15,000-strong military wing of the mainstream Supreme Council for the Islamic Revolution in Iraq headed by Abd al-Aziz al-Hakim—may also conduct operations against American troops. Finally, there are the small and isolated Wahabi terrorist cells of Ansar al-Islam and Ansar al-Sunna, groups that are said to have connections to al-Qaeda operatives like Abu Musab al-Zarqawi. Their actions, often using suicide bombers, are spectacular but do not make up the bulk of the resistance to the US-led occupation.

All pieces of the underground, by design or lack of it, operate in highly compartmentalized form: they don't use cell phones or computers and are thus hard to track electronically. They hold their meetings in mosques or moving cars. They pass messages by word of mouth. Their organizational cells operate on a need-to-know basis only.

Strategy for this diffuse collection of fighters is simple, almost intuitive. First, undermine the legitimacy and operations of the occupying powers by creating chaos and fear through sabotage and terror. Second, attack America's allies and the occupation's weak points so as to isolate the US. Third, attack and coopt Iraqi collaborators, like the police and the new National Guard. Fourth, kill and maim American troops to wear down the occupiers' morale. It's simple and brutal, but vast sections of world politics hinge on the outcome of this struggle.

The quest for the resistance in Adhamiya begins outside one of the local Internet cafés with some contacts among a clique of young men who play an online interactive video game called Netwar. The café is covered in tinted glass and nestled into the ground floor of a ramshackle building that looks like it was built in the 1920s or 1930s. Akeel knows some of the guys here from his prewar "student" days whiling away the hours as a cyber-assassin, gunning it out in the back alleys and bunkers of virtual cities under virtual occupation. Whenever these games pit "terrorists" against uniformed troops, these twenty-something middle-class sons of Baathists all vie for who gets to play the guerrillas. "I am really good at these games," says Akeel with a wistful twinkle in his eye.

After some bullshitting on the street corner out front, once the requisite meeting and greeting of old friends and the icebreaking jokes are done, Akeel and I peel off with one of the young men. He knows English fairly well, but Akeel tells him the score in Arabic. One can almost see the pride and adrenaline wash across the young man's face. He'll see what he can do; he has relatives who were high up in the military, plus he knows people who know people. This first meeting leads to others.

Eventually, I meet Abu Hassan, a thin, stern, chain-smoking former army captain who now imports machinery and with some of the profits funds resistance "operations." He wears a long dark *dishadasha,* a type of full-body shirt that falls to the ankles. We stroll down a side street and chat quickly.

"I have nothing to do with them," says Abu Hassan. I nod in understanding. But never mind that, the word is out: Abu Hassan is a key funder for the *mujahadeen* in this area and despite his claims that he lacks connections he says he might be able to introduce me to some of the fighters. I'm told to come back tomorrow.

At our first real sit-down meeting in a secure location, one of Abu Hassan's sons shows up with a pistol. The young man empties the gun's chambers into his palm and shows me the flat-tipped and highly destructive dum-dum bullets. Abu Hassan warns me to be completely honest about my identity and tells me to bring copies of the books I've written. "Otherwise some people might think you are CIA," he says with a smile. I am told that to meet the resistance I might be taken to Ramadi or Falluja.

That prospect doesn't sound safe. Akeel thinks it's a bluff. "They won't take us to Ramadi. They won't want to be in a car with a foreigner—there are too many checkpoints." True, there are now usually Iraqi police checkpoints on the roads in and out of Baghdad.

Our meetings with Abu Hassan are awkward but friendly. He is prone to abruptly changing the subject, switching suddenly from something heavy and political to something totally mundane and then, in a bit, back to issues about the resistance. At the next meeting, in the *diwan* or living room of a Baghdad house, a well-dressed older man arrives halfway through my strangely disjointed conversation with Abu Hassan. The man speaks English but won't give his name. He says he is a former general in the Iraqi army. Over little glasses of strong sweet tea, he tells me that he, too, is *not* connected to the resistance, but that he wants to see my books and be interviewed. What unfolds is a torrent of hurt pride, legitimate anti-Coalition critique, some wild lies and occasional sidebars of vitriol about the duplicity of the "collaborator" Shia.

"They lie to exaggerate their numbers," says the general. "All that you must do is go to the food program—every family is registered there—and count the Shia. They are not 60 percent. The Sunni are 53 percent, the Shia are 43 percent, and the rest are Christians and Kurds." The registration rolls of the World Food Program are a hot topic these days; many people say they could easily serve as the basis for election rolls. The CPA, wary of popular control and of Shia domination, denies this. As for the general's claims, he may in fact be correct about the number of Shia families on the food program rolls, but the Shia often registered as Sunni to avoid Saddam's repression.

"The Shia know nothing! The Sunni must govern Iraq," growls the ex-general. But his main grievance is America.

"We could not fight their weapons. They bombed us from the sky.

The Iraqi army was very strong, very important. It was very bad when America destroyed it!" The former general is on the edge of the couch, gesticulating, driving home his points with an intense, contained rage. Behind him on a TV screen, a black-and-white Cary Grant chatters away in silence.

Toward the end of the meeting the general's pretense of having no connection to the resistance seems to slip away: "We read Mao on guerrilla warfare. We are prepared. The war never stopped for us. We just came home and now fight in new ways." When the general leaves he takes the copies of my books from Abu Hassan.

For the next meeting my instructions are simple: go to a certain street corner and wait. Someone in a car will pick me up. The sky is a wet, wintry gray as Akeel and I arrive at the designated street corner. Akeel points to some nearby graffiti: "This one says, 'Death to all spies and collaborators.'" Nearby stands a well-dressed young man with close-cropped hair and a boxy leather jacket. He's holding a spiral notebook and looks like a typical twenty-one-year-old middle-class Iraqi college kid, but he is waiting for something and it's not a bus. His gaze always returns to fix on the two of us. The resistance is said to have "many eyes"; most cells retain scores of people who do nothing but watch and report on what they see.

"Man, do you realize this is fucking *crrrazy*?" says Akeel with a big grin. It does feel a bit sketchy at the moment. Then a black BMW pulls up. The driver is Abu Hassan, and I am relieved to see a familiar face.

"Get in," he says.

We drive fast and in silence away from the area where we were picked up. Abu Hassan is tense and smoking cigarettes. He again warns of the dangers. "If anything goes wrong they will find your hotel and kill you," he says, turning to look at me with an expression that is both threatening and concerned. Then he tells me to swear on the Bible, or, as Akeel, who is now very somber and contained, translates it, "the Christian book." "Swear that you are honest." From the plush back seat of the speeding BMW I swear to him that my intentions are honest.

By now the winter light has faded, night is falling across the city, and the electricity blinks out in large parts of northern Baghdad. After a circuitous trip through the dark city we stop at a side street. Abu Hassan bangs on the metal gate of an empty house. No answer. We move on and soon arrive in the cramped and muddy Adhamiya souk; its old streets, crowded with stalls, shops and garbage, are too narrow for US Humvees to enter. At one point the BMW's path is blocked by a truck unloading produce; Abu Hassan, looking like the prosperous Baghdadi burgher he is in his *de rigueur* winter-season leather jacket and dark pants, gets out and berates the truck's crew and they meekly move their vehicle. Back in the car he's bitter: "There is no respect," he says in English, then in Arabic, "This sort of thing never used to happen. The Americans have destroyed this country." Akeel translates quietly.

Further into the souk we stop in front of a shop whose lights are on thanks to a loud gasoline generator. Abu Hassan gets out without telling us what is happening, then returns with two small fluted glasses of hot lemon tea. He chats with a shopkeeper, but mostly he just waits around outside the car. Then we move out again, away from the generator-lit shops into the gloomy side streets, and stop to pick up a man whose face is wrapped in a *kaffia*. We keep driving.

The man, in his late forties, says he was a professional soldier and that he now runs a "team" of resistance fighters that has launched "many operations." He says he is fighting because the war shamed and destroyed a once proud army and because the occupation is abusing and humiliating Iraqis and Islam. The goal of his cell, which is made up of "less than twenty" local men, is to "repel the invaders and restore sovereignty." I ask if he expects to militarily defeat the US, or if the strategy is political. He explains the fundamental logic of asymmetrical warfare, stripped down to the raw essentials: "No, we will not drive them out with military means alone. We will kill American soldiers until the people in America get tired and bring them home."

Does his cell have a name, or is it part of any larger group? He pauses as the car lurches around a corner and then snaps, "We are *al-mujaha-deen*," using the generic term for holy warriors. "Elsewhere the fighters are called Muhammad's Army. But the names do not matter. We are all fighting for our country." He adds that "our leaders have contact with Saddam's Fedayeen," referring to the old regime's paramilitary terror squads and special forces trained in suicide tactics and directly loyal to Uday Hussein. When I ask about his group's theory or ideology he says, "We believe in the ideology of the Baath Party and of Islam." He says his men are mostly former soldiers. They are loyal to Saddam but they never took orders from him. Will Saddam's capture affect their fight?

"No, we will keep fighting. Our goals are clear. We want sovereignty. We will force the Americans to go home."

He claims that his team works with other cells on planning and executing larger attacks. He says that his team and one from al-Quds plus one from Ramadi were responsible for recent attacks in Karbala that killed some Thai soldiers, and that contrary to press reports no car bombs were used. "Some of our RPGs and small Katyusha rockets hit cars with gas in them and they exploded. Our real target was an American intelligence building on that base." At the time I don't think much of this comment, but several months later it turned out that contrary to the official story there was in fact a group of US soldiers and other operatives working with the international forces in Karbala. As for the Fedayeen, the masked fighter says they are still around, working on their own and, when they need to, with local cells like his.

He also claims that the Iraqi resistance had nothing to do with a recent suicide bombing that destroyed an upscale restaurant and killed several Iraqis. "We do not kill Iraqis, unless they are military interpreters or spies." And for these "traitors" his team maintains a "blacklist" of names, several of which have already been "crossed off"—that is, assassinated. To bolster his claim about not hurting Iraqis he points out sites around Adhamiya where there have clearly been IED explosions. "See, there are no shops here. The roads are wide."

He says that his group has "many eyes" working inside the police and in the new Iraqi army. This is totally believable since there are continual reports of Iraqi police and ICDC men firing on American patrols. The occupation's "puppet army" is a thoroughly booby-trapped tool: use it too aggressively and it might blow up. He won't specify whether any of his team have been killed or captured, but he says that many people in Adhamiya have been arrested.

When I ask about new American methods for jamming the frequencies used to trigger IEDs, he says, "We have our engineers. They use the remote controls of car-door locks and garage-door openers and other devices. Sometimes it is just wires." He says their bombs are usually made from disabled artillery rounds or plastic explosives molded with plaster to fit into walls or look like rocks. He says they work on finding ways to foil the American military's technology. "We are constantly changing our patterns."

It would be very difficult to prove or disprove this masked man's assertions, short of watching him in action. But the man's genuine nervousness, the ubiquitous but discreetly stashed pistols, and the real risk to any Iraqi who would pretend to be a guerrilla give credence to his claim of being a resistance leader.

As for the underground's structure and methods the man confirms a general picture that has been gleaned from other press accounts and recent military intelligence: the resistance is highly decentralized and is kept so by fear of spies and lack of secure communications. Often fighters are related and operate in units that are all kin. Other cells are more formal and maintain their anonymity from each other as much as possible by using *noms de guerre*. Cells operate in small networks or completely alone. Compartmentalization is their key to survival; it makes the underground forces resilient and hard to crush because it limits every US victory and inroad into the resistance. The military could bust this cell in Adhamiya and torture the truth from each of its members, but how far would the trail lead? Eventually the US forces would be back at square one: getting bombed and not knowing who was doing it.

In short, the mind of the resistance is everywhere; there is no head to cut off. Its strategy does not take the form of a plan but rather that of a logic or sensibility embedded in Iraqi culture: repel the invader. And this leaves American forces baffled, striking at shadows. Brigadier General Martin Dempsey of the 1st Armored Division, which controlled Baghdad for the first year of occupation, acknowledged this in one of his press conferences: "When we were looking at those cells, we were never sure exactly what existed above them ... We really didn't know how the cells in Adhamiya related to the cell in the Abu Ghraib [village] or the cell in the al-Jihad neighborhood."[2]

But compartmentalization and the ever-shifting horizontally organized networks of cells also limit the resistance's ability to coordinate large actions, build support networks, or even control its own cadre. If a guerrilla army is entirely informal, who is to stop fighters from dropping out or defecting at will? The strange dialectic of this real-life version of Netwar means that the underground's unique structure is both its greatest strength and greatest weakness.

After an hour or so Abu Hassan and the resistance fighter want to end the interview. I thank them and they drop Akeel and me off at the site of a recent IED blast in Adhamiya.

"Oh my God, we just interviewed the resistance," says Akeel, lighting a cigarette. We check out the IED blast, wander around the empty streets in an adrenaline-fueled euphoric daze congratulating each other on a job well done. Then as the damp chill begins to bite we sober up and realize that we should make our way to a main road, flag a cab and get the hell out of Dodge.

U ltimately, this meeting leaves the impression of a resistance that is ideologically and organizationally so fragmented as to verge on incoherence; it has superbly simple tactics and the perfect tools for guerrilla warfare but no clear strategy and no clear political vision other than the very broad teachings of Islam. The Sunni guerrillas are less a movement in the traditional sense than a collection of nationalists and soldiers with serious grievances, military training, and ready access to both weapons and targets.

Is this diffuse constellation of armed cells throughout the society a sign of success, the brilliance of asymmetrical warfare taken to a new level? Or is it a failure: the manifest *inability* of the resistance to be more organized, more united, and more politically coherent? As we look for a ride out of Adhamiya, it's hard to tell.

One thing is for sure: this is an insurgency that will be nearly impossible to crush. The resistance will never win militarily, but as the cell leader who rode with me in Abu Hassan's BMW explained, maybe it does not need to.

Reports from the western desert towns of Falluja, Khalidiyah and Ramadi paint a picture of a resistance that is perhaps slightly more Islamist but not necessarily of the Wahabi fundamentalist or the al-Qaeda variety. Here tribal affiliation is more important than in Baghdad, but at the same time the Baath Party and the old organs of state appear to play an important role in the resistance. Two pieces by the *Christian Science Monitor's* Nicholas Blandford profiled a resistance fighter who called himself Ahmed. He described an anonymous cell of local men, including many army veterans, who were inspired and led by local Sunni clerics, some of whom had secretly served with Muslim forces in Chechnya. The cell's leader, named Saad, would plan operations and pass on his instructions by word of mouth.

As Blandford described it: "The cell's members received little training. Ahmed served two years in the Iraqi Army and had been taught how to fire pistols, automatic rifles and light machine guns. Once in the resistance, a former army sergeant showed him how to fire a rocket-propelled grenade." But Ahmed never got to practice or actually fire the weapon until his first combat operation, and then he missed his target, a Humvee. US soldiers call this style of shooting "spray and pray."[3]

A report in *Iraq Today,* the country's (now-defunct) English-language paper, portrayed the resistance as somewhat more organized than most observers had thought. According to this description, the resistance, or at least some parts of it, operate with a higher level of organization in which the Fedayeen hard core serves as a link between exiled Baathist elites and the local cells. This fits with the Adhamiya cell leaders' cryptic comments about the Fedayeen playing a special role in the resistance.

According to the *Iraq Today* story, a Fedayeen fighter named Fathel described the formation of underground cells just after the war ended. Fathel's commander ordered him to send his family to safety and rent a house for himself outside Baghdad; his unit was to move to areas where they were not known, lie low and await orders, then resume operations as guerrillas. All of this he did. After Saddam's capture in early December 2003, Fathel was summoned to Amman where former leaders of the security forces had rented large houses. Fathel says that at a meeting of old Fedayeen comrades resistance leaders from Iraq were instructed to shift the focus of their attacks from US forces to "remove Iraqi people who were agents of the US."[4] January, February and March were indeed bloody months for the newly minted Iraqi security forces. As Mao recommended:

> In guerrilla warfare, select the tactic of seeming to come from the east and attacking from the west; avoid the solid, attack the hollow; attack; withdraw; deliver a lightning blow, seek a lightning decision. When guerrillas engage a stronger enemy, they withdraw when he advances; harass him when he stops; strike him when he is weary; pursue him when he withdraws. In guerrilla strategy, the enemy's rear, flanks, and other vulnerable spots are his vital points, and there he must be harassed, attacked, dispersed, exhausted and annihilated.

Clearly Saddam was not at the apex of any resistance movement. As one US intelligence official told the press, the notion that Saddam was in charge of the underground was "just flat wrong."[5] Nor was his capture followed by mass roundups, though there was a series of US offensives throughout the Sunni Triangle.

An April 2004 Pentagon study of the resistance painted a picture similar to the one supplied by *Iraq Today*. According to the *New York Times*, the report found that "Iraqi officers of the Special Operations and Anti-terrorism Branch, known within Saddam's government as M-14, are responsible for planning roadway improvised explosive devices and some of the larger car bombs that have killed Iraqis, Americans and other foreigners."[6] These findings were based on documents seized by the Iraq Survey Group and on the interrogation of high-ranking M-14 members in US custody.

Scott Ritter said pretty much the same thing in an article published months before the Pentagon report appeared. Ritter said that as a weapons inspector he had seen prewar evidence of planning for a postinvasion guerrilla war while searching the premises of an organization known as M-21, the Special Operations Directorate of the Iraqi Intelligence Service. Ritter's account is worth quoting at length:

> While I found no evidence of WMDs, I did find an organization that specialized in the construction and employment of "improvised explosive devices"—the same IEDs that are now killing Americans daily in Iraq.
>
> When we entered the compound, three Iraqis tried to escape over a wall with documents, but they were caught and surrendered the papers. Like reams of other documents stacked inside the buildings, these papers dealt with IEDs. I held in my hands a photocopied primer on how to conduct a roadside ambush using IEDs, and others on how to construct IEDs from conventional high explosives and military munitions.
>
> The sophisticated plans—albeit with crude drawings—showed how to take out a convoy by disguising an IED and when and where to detonate it for maximum damage.

Then at another facility,

> I saw classrooms for training all Iraqi covert agents in the black art of making and using IEDs. My notes recall tables piled with mockups of mines

and grenades disguised in dolls, stuffed animals, and food containers—and classrooms for training in making car bombs and recruiting proxy agents for using explosives.[7]

All of this summons the image of a profoundly determined foe that, even prior to the invasion, anticipated and accepted a long period of guerrilla warfare. No doubt when the intelligence nets haul up informational detritus like this it must cause the blood to run cold in the veins of the smarter spooks and military planners.

And how do the guerrillas supply themselves? Getting weapons—one of the primary difficulties faced by most insurgencies—is not a problem in Iraq. Central Iraq is absolutely littered with weapons: some were hidden before the war, some were just dumped when Saddam's army melted away in April 2003. As one report put it, "The rapid capitulation of Hussein's regime also left the best part of two divisions intact north of Baghdad, untouched by the [US] 4th Infantry Division's stalled pincer sweep from the north." This alone meant an estimated "350,000 tons of ammunition is unaccounted for."[8]

In the early days of the resistance there were also millions of dollars in cash in the hands of former intelligence officers or stashed with the weapons. The US military has seized much of this money, but the underground's methods are quite low-cost just as they are low-tech.

The danger of meeting the resistance was pointed out to me by a journalist whom I respect very much. On the way back into Iraq for my winter trip, traveling with my friend and fellow journalist Rob Eshelman, I by chance ran into Rajiv Chandrasekaran of the *Washington Post*. I first met Chandrasekaran just after the Karrada Street firefight. He was on the security perimeter as we were leaving and the site was being cleaned up. I was high on adrenaline, in a nasty mood, and I had been rather rude in answering his questions. Chandrasekaran had been a complete gentleman and when we met again he didn't remember me as being an asshole. "Wow, was that in August?" he said. "That's when things really started to go haywire. It's all blurred together at this point."

Chandrasekaran explained that, for the moment, he and his colleague Anthony Shadid had decided to steer clear of direct contacts with the resistance and had instead focused on reconstructing the biographies of dead resistance fighters. This is a more reliable way of discovering who the rebels really are.

"We think meeting with these guys is actually quite dangerous. It's not out of the question that they'll pull a Danny Pearl—you know, start kidnapping and killing journalists. It's not like that hasn't happened in this region before." Several months later that's exactly what starts, at least the kidnapping part. One victim was my old friend David Martinez, a filmmaker from San Francisco and Austin who was held for a day by the resistance outside Falluja.

At the same pit stop where I talk with Chandrasekaran I meet the inimitable David Rieff, who writes for the *New York Times Magazine;* he is also the son of Susan Sontag. Tall and immaculately dressed, Rieff looks like Frank Zappa as fastidious intellectual. Adorned in heavy Santa Fe–style turquoise jewelry, sporting a big mane of silvered black hair and a finely sculpted goatee, he wears a small, neatly folded *kaffia* draped over his shoulders like a tennis towel.

Rieff has a totally different view of the resistance. In a languid and nasal tone he explains that the Bush administration "doesn't have an Iraq problem, they have a Baghdad problem. Or a Tikrit-to-Baquba-to-Ramadi problem." Maybe he's right, I thought. After all, this was early winter—before the Mahdi Army rebellion and the siege of Falluja.

"Who are the resistance?" asks Rieff rhetorically. "They have no leader, no demands, no clear organization. They are a nuisance, sure. It's awful for the families of those killed. But does it really mean very much?" With that Rieff reaches under his windbreaker into his suit jacket, producing a little cylindrical metal container cast to look like a stack of old coins, unscrews the top, retrieves a brightly colored pharmaceutical, and ends his statement by putting the pill on his tongue and washing it down with bottled water.

As the Rieff–Chandrasekaran convoy drives away, Eshelman and I watch in silence. "That was weird," says Eshelman, face blank, hands thrust deep in his pockets against the chill desert wind.

A t a farm on the muddy floodplains near Balad, a provincial town about an hour north of Baghdad, Akeel and I managed one more meeting with the resistance, this time with a rural cell that has no connection to the one in Adhamiya. These men are farmers, all brothers or cousins and devout Sufis. They claim to have momentarily halted their fight against the Americans; they will give the occupiers one last chance. "Maybe they will fix the roads. We will see."

I spend a long time by the river talking to one of the brothers about what the Americans have done here and about farming. He grows cucumbers, eggplants, dates, "everything." Then we move inside to the *diwan* and sit on cushions, and slowly the rest of his crew shows up. Cross-legged on the floor of the cold farmhouse we wait for a lunch of fried chicken, rice and soup. As usual, the women are behind a wall, cooking and watching the children. The man from the riverbank explains, "My brothers and I did many operations against the Americans, but it is dangerous to talk about this. We spent a lot of money on remote controls."

In these tightly knit villages, the resistance seems to be even more informally structured than the networked cells in Adhamiya. "Sometimes a group of brothers or cousins will do an action," explains the former fighter. "Or maybe someone from [the nearby village of] Abu Hishma might ask you to help with an action. You'll go to a field and you will find, maybe, some of your friends and maybe other people who you don't know." He says that fear and religious differences have kept this network of overlapping cells from uniting.

According to this young farmer and his brothers, the guerrillas around Balad all have different reasons for fighting. Some fight for Islam, some for Saddam, some just to get the Americans out, and some for revenge. These young men seem to have fought for all of the above: they lost their father to an American bomb, they feel humiliated by the occupation, they are intensely religious, and a few of them really like Saddam.

So why have they stopped their attacks in the last few weeks? The young man doing most of the talking thinks for a bit, then, revealing the deep war-weariness of many Iraqis, says, "It's hard to fight and kill other people." He adds: "The Americans are very brutal, they are monsters. They have killed whole families and arrested a quarter of the men in this area." Indeed, US pressure is intense: American troops conduct some 1,400 patrols and raids across Iraq every day.[9] And there is a notoriously tough US colonel, Nathan Sassaman, running counterinsurgency in this area. Along with delivering severe repression, he has promised some real reconstruction.

And then, as if on cue, two deafeningly loud and very intimidating Apache helicopter gunships sweep low over the farm. "Last night they were shooting at the other bank of the river," says one of the men.

Just before lunch is served and the political talk winds down, the for-

mer guerrilla concludes, "Perhaps the resistance is just resting, waiting to
see what the Americans will do next." A young boy unrolls a plastic sheet
on the carpeted floor and then brings in heaping plates of fried chicken,
rice, pickles, salad and bean soup. Other than the soup, we eat from communal plates with pieces of crisp, leathery flatbread fresh from an oven
hidden somewhere back in the women's part of the house.

Returning to Baghdad it is clear that while some in the underground
may be giving up, the war is still in full effect. Three truckers working
for the Coalition Provisional Authority have been shot; one was killed.
A week or so later, another huge car bomb goes off at the aptly named
"Assassin's Gate," one of the main entrances to the Coalition's fortress
"Green Zone." Racing through a gloomy morning of thick, cold smog,
David Martinez and I get to the blast area just as American troops are
pushing back the first wave of reporters. The bomb has killed more than
twenty and wounded close to sixty. It is the usual hellish scene of gore
and wreckage. The party, or cell, that set off this bomb has released no
statement, made no demands. But the brutal semiotics are clear: among
the casualties are three US soldiers and three American contractors; the
rest were all Iraqis who, whether as maids or managers, worked with the
Coalition.

6

Voyeur's Banquet: Dead People for Breakfast and Dinner

> If your pictures aren't good enough, you aren't close enough.
> Robert Capa

The explosion hits just as our omelets arrive and just as Crazy Dave, the trilingual daredevil-cum-"journalist," is launching into his morning soliloquy. It is something about the Frankfurt School and the Taliban. In many ways it is a typical morning at the Hotel Agadeer—an eight-story budget hotel filled with Iranian Shiite pilgrims, Bangladeshi construction workers, and about a twenty or so European and American freelancers, filmmakers and assorted nutjobs. The Iranian pilgrims had all eaten their complimentary breakfasts and loaded into their aging Mercedes buses to head for the holy cities. Now, at eight o'clock, the crews of coffee-starved Eastern European, American, French and Italian journalists roll in and meet up with their Iraqi colleagues, the translators and drivers. But that morning the wake-up process skips to fast-forward.

In mid-sentence the air shakes and conversation is brought to a stunned halt by a forceful sonic jolt. Two blocks away a small convoy of US Humvees has been hit by a powerful IED. From across the dining room our postblast trance is broken. "That's close!" booms Attila, a longtime war correspondent from Hungary who rules the roost. He is in the doorway as if he'd been waiting for this moment all along.

"Let's go!" His roar is that of a coach: encouraging, concerned and slightly disappointed. We dash up eight flights to the roof, with each complement of crumbling marble steps sucking in the gas fumes that emanate up from the generator in the basement and fill the hotel's stairway.

"Look! On Karrada!" shouts Attila. "You can see the people running." Down we plunge, jumping the stairs three and four at a time and then running down the block.

It's a four-Humvee convoy, two blocks away. The IED was plastered into the concrete median strip and went off between the last two vehicles, blowing out their windshields and scattering shrapnel and concrete for yards in every direction, wounding several. The street is filling fast, and pandemonium reigns. A crowd of men has formed. Some are tending to the wounded, others are yelling for help, yelling for people to get out of the way, yelling for God. One man is clearly dead, lying on his back in the street, blood spreading around him. Journalists start arriving, joining the freak show from the Agadeer; some people snap stills, and Attila has his video camera hoisted high. The soldiers are yelling, trying to clear a perimeter around the dead man.

"Get back! Get back! Hey, I got a job to do," shouts the staff sergeant in charge. Then he pats his M-4 with a gloved hand: "You know what'll happen if shit gets out of control. So please: Get back!"

It is no use: the crowd closes in. They're angry, yelling at the soldiers, standing defiantly in front of the rifles. Others close in around the dead man; someone covers him with a cloth advertising banner, painted in Arabic script. Bloods seeps through and pools up around the corpse. Soon the dazed staff sergeant orders the squad to move their vehicles fifty yards up the street. The crowd takes the corpse.

A shaken older man wearing glasses and a leather coat, blood running from his hand, approaches and volunteers his account: the bomb went off, and then he hit the ground. He got up and everything around him was smashed. Now he's bleeding. His name is Abdul. He is an engineer for the city, working on street repairs. He is trembling.

I am getting worried that someone will suck one of us journos deep into the crowd for a beat-down. Then I start anticipating a secondary blast. We'll all be ripped to shreds; I can feel it, and my skin tingles in anticipation. Then this wave of fear washes back out into the ever-present, bigger pool of fear, the shark tank, that is just part of Iraq's emotional landscape. I move up to the soldiers and ask what happened.

"Was that an IED in the median?"

"Affirmative, one dead and our interpreter wounded, with protruding fractures on the collarbone and forearm," answers the super-amped squad medic.

"Hey, Callahan! Come on!" yells the staff sergeant, pointing with two fingers to his eyes and then the rooftops. The semaphore is clear: your 15 minutes of fame are over! Shut up and watch for snipers!

Out of nowhere—but perhaps not surprisingly, since this is a country that has weathered three major wars in twenty years and is still at war now—a simple wood coffin appears and the dead man is placed in it. The coffin is hoisted aloft and the crowd carries it a half-block down the street to a small mosque, chanting "Allahu Akbar, Allahu Akbar."

"C.P., you know, I walked right past that spot ten minutes before the bomb went off," says Akeel. He had spent the night with his future wife, a crazy social worker/activist from Birmingham who has set up a shelter for Baghdadi street kids and takes pleasure in verbally harassing US troops whenever possible. (Weeks later, a moneychanger on the same corner tells

Akeel, "I feel like I killed that man. He asked me where a certain office was, and I pointed it out to him and then he crossed the street. The bomb went off and he was killed.")

Everyone gets a thrill from these near-miss events. It's not just the adrenaline: there's also a dirty survivor's euphoria. But these quotidian tragedies are of course profoundly depressing and have a way of stripping any hopeful meaning out of the political "big picture."

"Got some good close-ups of the dead guy, lifted the sheet." It's Crazy Dave. When we went to the roof he disappeared to the street, and now he has popped up, as he often does at such moments, to offer some bit of bad news or madness.

"Dave, you're sick."

No firefight follows the attack; it's a "single element" engagement, so eventually it's back to the hotel. Our eggs are waiting, cold but covered with clean plates. The headwaiter welcomes us back with a flat smile and fresh tea.

"Just like Sarajevo," laughs Attila upon seeing that breakfast has resumed. The coach is pleased.

On one level the Hotel Agadeer is an anomaly, a strangely bohemian oasis in the largely square, center-right, big-money journalism scene that rules the press space in Baghdad. But the Agadeer is also tainted by all the parasitic voyeurism and licentious careerism of any other imperial war press pool.

For much of my time in Iraq the Agadeer was home. It was in its own way a little village within the sprawling mess of Baghdad. Unlike the mainstream journalists, who were usually boring and polite Ivy Leaguers, the cast at the Agadeer was made up of eccentrics.

Enter the Agadeer's small, dark, mirrored lobby and at the desk you meet Baba, an intense and thoughtful man. In his late forties, Baba has gray hair and weary pale-blue eyes. He is fluent in English, remembers everyone's name, and is always watching out for us: "Be careful out there." "Christian, are your friends back from Falluja?" Baba had been a merchant, but when looters emptied his shoe shop during "liberation" he was forced to take work at the Agadeer and suffer under the hotel's tyrannical skinflint of a manager.

"This is the freedom," sighs Baba, peering out across a haze of freshly exhaled smoke. Outside the traffic is in gridlock because of a checkpoint or cordon search up the road. (Although we didn't know it at the time, Baba's wife was dying of brain cancer. He would later blame her illness on tomatoes from Basra contaminated with depleted uranium.)

Across from the desk in a low overstuffed chair is Mister Khalial, a Jordanian "businessman" who is invariably clad in a dark-blue Armani and tie or a beige velour tracksuit. His hands are always occupied with a cigarette, a coffee or amber-colored plastic worry beads. The right side of Mister Khalial's face bears a huge and dramatic scar, the type left by saber slashes across the cheeks of Hollywood bad guys. I never had the presence of mind to ask how he came by that memento. At midday, one might find Mister Khalial meeting with nattily clad sheikhs in the second-floor dining room alcove, but usually he is just hanging around the lobby, smoking, flipping his beads, watching people come and go. Then sometimes he shows up in a café across town, near a cordon search, or at a demonstration, always watching, always patient, always friendly, but always distant.

"You think Mister Khalial is a spook?" someone once asked us incredulously.

"No, I just want to know why Mister Khalial always happens to be where we happen to be," explains David Martinez, a filmmaker, activist and fast-talking, wisecracking old friend of mine from San Francisco.

Upstairs live the journalists. There is the ubiquitous Crazy Dave, known to us as David Michael—that is, until he skips out on a fifty-dollar hotel tab and Baba tells us that his passport gives his name as David Stahl. Crazy Dave is the type one wants to dislike but ends up appreciating anyway. I like him because he is smart: he reads books. The scion of "an international banking family," as he puts it, Dave was raised in France and educated at Berkeley. For the last eight years he had been traveling in war zones: northern Cambodia with the still-armed Khmer Rouge, then Afghanistan under the Taliban and then in Afghanistan again when it came under US control. Now he is here with us, sent like some giant avenging mosquito to camp out on the war-frayed nerves of low-budget freelancers.

Usually Dave stays in a one-dollar-a-night rat-infested dive nearby—he bragged endlessly about the hardship—but at times he sleeps on a couch in the lobby of the Agadeer. Crazy Dave is one of four guys at the Agadeer named David, the youngest being a thirteen-year-old Assyrian Christian street kid named Daud. He doesn't live at the hotel, but hangs out there all the time. Best of all, Daud is not actually a street kid: he lives nearby with his middle-class uncle, who has even bought him a Nintendo set. In reality Daud is just a rambunctious, devious little ruffian who enjoys conning gullible honkies by claiming that he is a glue-sniffing street urchin. He has what he claims is a bullet scar on his head.

A guy named Aaron—we call him "Aaron the art capitalist"—had given Daud a camera and asked the boy to shoot short films of life in Baghdad. Aaron promised he'd send money back to Iraq if Daud would give the tapes to the concierge at the Palestine Hotel, who would then DHL them to Aaron's loft in New York City's DUMBO neighborhood. Daud would end all his video reports with the dramatic newsy signoff: "Daud, dis Baghdad."

Then there is Dahr Jamail: brave, sober, honest and hardworking, he is

a lefty Alaskan now but was originally from a right-wing family in Texas
of Lebanese descent. Dahr had been a mountain rescue paramedic who
worked on contract with the Forest Service and the National Park Service
in Alaska. This trip to Iraq is his first foray into journalism: the horizontal
mountain of information and narrative and lies. Like many freelancer writ-
ers he can fall into angry moods, worn down by the deadlines, logistics,
money problems and routine fear. But Dahr became one of my closest and
most trusted friends in Iraq.

For a while Dahr's roommate is a Hungarian guy named Mihaly
Meszaros, whom we call Meshi. Thin and angular with slicked-back black
hair and a black beard, Meshi speaks with the accent and slow cadence of
Count Dracula—not surprisingly, since he is originally from Transylvania,
near the Romanian border. A devout Muslim, except when he guiltily sips
an occasional beer, he reads the Koran at night. Ask him what he is up to
and he explains apologetically in his Count Dracula accent that he is "making rrreally crrrap movies, toe-tal-ly crrrap'" about things like Baghdad's
Arnold Schwarzenegger Bodybuilding Club, which is near the BBC compound. "It is toe-tal-ly stupid. But diz iz what my bozz wants. So, I shoot
da footage for him."

Down the hall is the crew from Radio Polskia, Tomas and Michael. Tomas is tall and blond, wears silk scarves and undresses young men with his
eyes. He is the flamboyant flying ace of Polish Radio. "I have a weakness for
porcelain," he once confessed. "Old porcelain I collect it compulsively. Do
you like it? Some of it here is very nice." He says stuff like this, then sizes
you up flirtatiously and heads off to find the bang-bang.

His colleague Michael looks like he just stepped off the streets of Green-
point, Brooklyn, decked out in a hooded sweatshirt, baseball hat and baggy
jeans. Under the brim of his Radio Polskia cap his eyes are dark and baggy with fatigue. In Poland he had hosted a talk show about cars. How he

ended up in Iraq was always unclear, even to him. Michael knows that the situation around him is profoundly unhealthy, and after several months of filing two stories a day he is ready to split back to Poland. But his departure for home is delayed at the last minute. After a raucous going-away party, a drunk Romanian journalist, also named Michael, runs an Iraqi police checkpoint in Radio Polskia's little Mitsubishi SUV. The Iraqi cops shoot up the SUV but amazingly do not hit Romanian Michael, who is nevertheless hospitalized for injuries sustained when he lost control of the vehicle. Radio Polskia Michael is forced to stick around and deal with the fallout.

The top floor of the Agadeer is the domain of the laundry room, where two Iraqi men, Muhammad and Qassim, spend their days manning ancient industrial washers, folding towels or reading the papers. Next to their engine room of suds and cloth is Suite 800—the Agadeer's control tower, home to Attila, our unofficial leader.

Tall and big-bellied with a frowning, fleshy mug, Attila Penzreicki has a penchant for cheap Iraqi silver and leather jackets. He peers at the world through tiny square-rimmed glasses that make him look all the more like a sullen caged bear. He sells stories to pretty much all of his homeland's radio, TV and print media. When the news is slow he also sells cheap Iraqi silver to the Hungarian soldiers billeted in Hilla, a town about an hour southwest of Baghdad. Mister Khalial calls Attila "the sheikh of journalists." Dahr calls him "the ogre."

Attila had come to Iraq just after the conquest and found the Agadeer as it was reopening. He claimed the top floor as his lair, and on the roof he set up satellite dishes and would rent DSL Internet access to whoever wanted it; he would just drop a length of cable over the side of the hotel and down four, five or six stories to the rooms below.

While still in college at age twenty-one Attila left his native Budapest for Yugoslavia to document the meltdown of that country firsthand. For the next thirteen years he pursued war, skipping from the Balkans to Turkish Kurdistan to Rwanda, Sierra Leone, Nigeria and Kosovo. He's been under fire too many times to count. His stories, bitter and tragic, are doled out with a feigned reluctance. He says that his two worst moments were getting caught in crossfire while traversing the river between Burundi and Rwanda and seeing a friend of his get shot in the head by a sniper during a supposed cease-fire in Croatia. "We had to collect his stuff," says Attila, recounting that awful day. "In his jacket he had letters from his kids and wife. That is when it really hits you."

Attila's speech is clipped, sharp and heavily accented. He sounds like he is yelling, no matter the actual volume of his voice. "Are we on holiday? Or are we journalists?!" When the mayhem slows down, Attila gets depressed. He sulks around, chain-smoking in silence. At such moments he confesses that being a war correspondent is morally corrosive.

Sometime in the mid-nineties he had come upon a massive car accident in Hungary and immediately started taking photographs. Several minutes of snapping shots passed before he remembered that he had a cell phone, one of the few available in Hungary at the time. The fact that his first instinct had been to harvest images from the carnage rather than help the wounded with a call for emergency services had sickened him, and he swore he'd quit journalism. He resigned his job and got in his car to go on vacation, but the holiday turned into a road trip back to war-torn Yugoslavia. Like a junkie's solemn resolutions to stay away from needles and dope, Attila's recovery is always getting postponed for "just one last time."

Attila "has the aura." He goes places in Iraq that even the bravest translators and drivers refuse to visit—for example, he raced into an armed nighttime protest in Adhamiya for a funeral procession attended by a company of grenade-wielding Fedayeen. When there is mortaring or rocket attacks in the south of Baghdad Attila rushes into the night looking for the action.

When shooting or bomb blasts of any kind occur, Attila leads the charge. But when Dahr and I try to get him to climb the ancient spiraled minaret of the Abbasid Mosque in Samarra he declines. "I am afraid of heights. Ever zince I fell to zee bottom of a cave in zee Czech Republic and broke my leg."

The other key location at the Agadeer is a two-room suite called Room 100, home to my old friends Rob Eshelman and David Martinez, both lately of San Francisco. David is lugging around cameras for a Spanish TV crew and shooting footage for a documentary of his own. Rob is pitching stories to lefty rags in the United States. Bunking with them is a very French Trotskyist peace activist named Thomas. We joke that Thomas is so French that he looks like he is smoking a cigarette even when he isn't.

Also a frequent guest in Room 100 is Akeel, my translator and friend. Akeel is in many ways a sad barometer of the situation in Iraq: in the summer when we worked together he was professional and diligent. By winter he is devolving into heavy drinking and self-deluding despair. This isn't helped by the fact that most of the journalists he has worked with regularly collect horror stories. "There's a family out in Ramadi, they say US troops executed the father and two brothers. Wanna check it out?" How much of that can a man take?

I notice another change in him as well. When we first met in August 2003, he disliked Saddam—"Fuck Saddam. He stole from my people." By January Akeel inexplicably loves Saddam. "I really like his personality. And you know, he was so smart." When Saddam was captured Akeel broke down in tears. "It was like all of Iraq had been humiliated." This is all the more bizarre because some of Akeel's family had been badly treated by Saddam.

A young man close to Akeel, who also worked as a translator on occasion, had been press-ganged into the Fedayeen, a paramilitary terror-force run by Uday Hussein. The man in question, whom I interviewed at length, had been forced to watch innocent people thrown from helicopters, put through a brutal survival course in the desert, and trained to be a suicide bomber. Eventually the tormented young man, then only in his late teens, shot himself in the knee in hope of a medical discharge. His officers instead accused him of being a spy and jailed him for thirty-two days, during which he was tortured and sexually humiliated: his captors put out lit cigarettes on his arms and threatened to electrocute him. After a month they realized their captive was not an enemy spook, just a teenager desperate for a normal life, and they released him.

Another habitué of Room 100 is the young, quick-witted Dave Enders. He showed up in Baghdad just after the conquest and helped start a newspaper called *Baghdad Bulletin*. When that venture crashed and burned he stayed on to freelance and did some great reporting (such as exposing abuse at Abu Ghraib prison many months before the infamous photos were leaked). Only twenty-three years old, ambitious and well-educated, Enders is the sort of young man one might expect to be arrogant and competitively insecure, especially around a crew of guys ten years his senior. But quite the opposite, Enders is relaxed and generous.

Most of the guests at the Agadeer were Iranian pilgrims. These sojourners are an increasingly important part of the Iraqi landscape. As a Shiite state, Iran is full of people who want to visit the holy sites of the Shia faith, which are in Iraq, where the most important of the figures of Shiite Islam—the first twelve caliphs, descendants of the prophet Muhammad, starting with Imam Ali through to Imam Hussein and others—led the faith and were then usually murdered with swords or knives. Since the US conquest, Iraq's borders have opened and what was, according to the Iraqi paper *Al-Shira*, once an officially regulated flow of 500 Iranian pilgrims a day had by the beginning of 2004 surged to more than 3,000 pilgrims crossing into Iraq daily. Some reports indicate that this semi-legal and illegal flow of pilgrims is aided by members of the Islamic Dawa Party and the Supreme Council for the Islamic Revolution in Iraq (SCIRI) led by Iraqi Governing Council member Al-Bakr Hakim. For a mere fifty dollars, it is said, Shiite activists and militias ferry pilgrims past official border posts and into the holy cities of Najaf and Karbala, south of Baghdad. "It is chaos. Anyone can come in and we can't control this," complained the head of a customs post on Iraq's eastern border.[1]

The pilgrims at the Agadeer are not only not Iraqi and not Arab, they are also not urban, not young and not well traveled. From what we can glean, they are all middling peasants who had saved and scraped for years so they could visit the Shia holy cities. The men are wizened and hunched, thick-limbed and short, never taller than five-five. All of them wear the same uniform: sweater vests underneath a beat-up dark suit coat, loose dark pants and dark wool caps. Their facial hair ranges from mustaches with thick, graying shadows to full beards. The women are even shorter, just as weather-beaten, and all wear headscarves and *abayas,* the head-to-toe black robes preferred by conservative Shiite women. Invariably the ladies carry battered plastic thermoses of tea.

Frequently these travelers, out of their element in the extreme and having trouble with urban gadgets like elevators, mistake foreign journalists for hotel staff. It is not uncommon for some Iranian grandmother to stop you in the hallway and demand in a rural Farsi dialect that you help her open a door or make the elevator work. They never gesture or pantomime their requests, they just keeping speaking Farsi and expecting a journalist or Iraqi hotel porter to understand. Akeel would playfully make fun of them, calling them "Sharugees," a rather derogatory slang term for the Shia of southern Iraq.

New Year's Eve has arrived. The night is clear, and the sky is criss-crossed with the gently arcing tracer rounds from bursts of celebratory gunfire. Below, the city is calm but tense. Everyone waits for "something big." There are several parties under way for journos and NGOers and other occupiers. We pass on an invitation to the BBC's compound and instead head to an apartment we call the Italian embassy, which is really just the offices of an Italian NGO.

Before long the inevitable arrives in the form of a huge explosion with a dense angry core and wide rumbling echo. Attila and his translator Hamudi are the first to their feet. The blast was a kilometer to our east, but it was so loud that we're all disoriented. Some people think it came from behind us, others from out front. Again, we race to the roof scanning the night sky for smoke, then down to the cars. Six of us cram into Attila and Hamudi's sedan. Hamudi races the almost empty streets, the very embodiment of speed; Attila barks directions that are occasionally followed, usually ignored. First up to Sadoon Street; then, as ambulances and Iraqi police cars pass, we sweep back in pursuit through a police checkpoint flashing our press passes and shouting "Sahafee! Sahafee!" (Journalists).

Suddenly we arrive at the remains of the upscale Nabil restaurant just as the first medics unload. A car bomb has killed eight and wounded thirty-five. The scene is Armageddon in miniature. Illuminated by orange flame, the surrounding streets are strewn with debris: twisted metal, broken glass, part of a tweed jacket, a steering rod, half of a severed human foot with toes.

A thick torrent of flame streams from a thirty-foot depression in the side of the building, shattered glass coats the area, parked cars are leaking fuel, some of which ignites. All around windows are blown out. Again the push and pull between cops and the press, then soldiers and the press. Amidst the mayhem a woman sobs and pushes toward the restaurant. A man wanders dazed and bloody with a cloth dinner napkin pressed to his head. Two Iraqi firefighters mount the heap of rubble closest to the blaze and spray a weak stream of water into the fiery pit. The whole scene is lit orange by flame, then obscured, then revealed in orange again to form a chaotic visual loop.

Amidst it all is a tall man, the spitting image of Mexican president Vicente Fox, constantly moving from place to place. Each time he comes to rest he is bathed in the glow of TV spotlights. It's the new chief of police, and this is his media début. A blonde female TV journalist in a light-blue flak vest is the only person not moving around; she stares intently into her crew's camera and floodlights, waiting to go live.

Crazy Dave, whom I haven't seen in days, pops up. "Hey, dude. I got inside. Got good shots of the bodies. Mostly just legs sticking out of rubble. There are, like, bottles of fine wine and silverware all over the place. It's weird. Reuters might buy the tape."

An hour and a half after the blast and we're back at "the Italian embassy" drinking and eating while the music blares. Then at midnight it's back to the roof to watch the sky fill with tracer rounds. A woman at the party, Simone, exudes a charmed air. She seems to float around kissing everyone, wishing them a happy new year. On her way to the party, she "by chance" stopped at the Nabil for a drink—"just an apéritif." Forty minutes after she left the restaurant was blown to pieces. Now Simone is high on the bacchanalian war drug, a cocktail of luck, denial and ego. As an NGOer who must deal with the Baghdad cops on a regular basis, Simone has missed three bombings by less than an hour. "Happy New Year!" she says with a grin and a kiss.

The drinking and dancing will go on all night. "Very *haram*-a-rama," says Dave Martinez, playing on the Arabic word *haram,* meaning forbidden. Attila must file his story, so he and I head back to the Agadeer. Trying to sleep,

I watch the bullets streak across the sky. The outer wall of my room is plate glass. Finally, it's too much: all I can think about are AK rounds smashing through the glass and into my guts. Feeling ridiculous, I open the sides of my flak vest and lay it across my body lengthwise like a short Kevlar blanket. I prop one of the removable ceramic plates up to block the side of my head and take two Valium. Slowly, slowly, I fall asleep, images of the Nabil fading in and out.

In late March, the Mount Lebanon Hotel was bombed. The blast blew out windows at the nearby Agadeer. I was gone by then, but my colleague Naomi Klein passed on some of the details. Her room at the Adageer was flooded with dust and broken glass from the blast. After that the management asked all the foreigners to leave. Their presence was just too big a risk. Then the Shia rose up and journalists started getting kidnapped. (Dave Martinez was captured by the local *mujahadeen* outside Falluja, but luckily was released after a day.)

Attila also ran into trouble, but of a different sort. His debts finally caught up with him. He owed his translator, he owed Martinez, he owed a local store, and he owed who knows how many others. So Attila quietly left for Budapest. It was, in many ways, a sadly fitting end to one little piece of the colonial circus in Iraq.

7

From Dreamland to Falluja

We fought a military war; our opponents fought a political one. We sought physical attrition; our opponents aimed for our psychological exhaustion. In the process, we lost sight of one of the cardinal maxims of guerrilla warfare: the guerrilla wins if he does not lose. The conventional army loses if it does not win.

Henry Kissinger on the Vietnam War

It's a cool winter afternoon in January 2004 and Operation Dozer, a large-scale incursion into the city of Falluja, is taking longer than expected—much longer. Instead of lasting two or three hours, Dozer has lasted all day, and when the 82nd Airborne spends any extended period of time in Falluja they get attacked. The mission is named for the bulldozer that is clearing away some guardrails and a mangled statue along one of the city's main thoroughfares. The resistance has been packing the backs of the rails with plastic explosives and using the broken statue to triangulate on passing convoys and time the detonation of their IEDs. One IED in this area killed a GI, Sergeant Paul Johnson, and wounded seven others a few months ago. So in a slow, clumsy, bureaucratic way, this operation is payback.

"Man, *this* is turning into a cluster fuck," quips a paratrooper with the

82nd. He is perched in the back of a Humvee, looking down the barrel of an M-249 SAW; he's pulling security, watching the perimeter. Strapped to his body armor is a small, fist-sized brown teddy bear. Behind him a squad of soldiers is strung out along the street crouching or leaning on walls, peering around corners. Other squads are searching houses, going through the bedclothes, rifling the cabinets, routing among construction supplies in the courtyards, looking for weapons, IED materials and "bad guys." Overhead in the empty blue sky two small Kiowa choppers skim the rooftops looking for snipers.

All around, but at a distance, stand small and defiant clusters of Fallujan men, smirking or glaring at the US troops. A boy of about nine approaches an intelligence officer standing nearby and with handsigns demands the soldier's mirrored sunglasses. "No fucking way, brat," the officer responds. The day is bright, cool and crisp, but looking around one gets the sense that it can only end badly.

We are an hour outside of central Baghdad at the heart of Iraq's "security riddle"—the north side of Falluja in the restive province of al-Anbar, aka "the wild west." The locals call this neighborhood al-Askari (literally "the officers' neighborhood"). The 82nd Airborne's satellite photomaps have it marked with the moniker "Queens." Other parts of town are called Manhattan, Brooklyn, Staten Island and the Bronx.

Al-Anbar province is one of Iraq's most culturally traditional and deeply religious regions. Here you can readily feel and taste how profoundly unprepared the US government is for its new role as overlord of the desert. To understand the war in these parts, you must first grasp a bit of al-Anbar's physical and social geography.

Falluja is at the eastern edge of the province and lies on a bend in the Euphrates among fertile and rich floodplains hemmed in by vast desiccated wastelands. Here the river runs eastward in its otherwise southerly course from Turkey and Syria through Iraq to the Gulf. The fertile part of al-Anbar running up along the Euphrates toward Syria is called the Shammar, but most of this heavily Sunni province is sun-blasted desert: its boundaries reach north and west to Syria and Jordan and south to Saudi Arabia. Here Iraq's tribes, which are more accurately described as large extended clans, still exercise considerable power, just as they have for millennia, regardless of who was titular master of their lands. The desert's harsh, impoverishing climate of searing heat in summer, bitter cold in winter, unrelenting wind and constant dust helped give the Bedouin tribes here a relative autonomy that no state has ever fully eradicated. Even today there are families that roam the desert largely ignoring the national borders that parse their homeland into Saudi Arabia, Iraq, Jordan and Syria. A similar disregard for state authority infuses the settled culture of the towns and provincial cities.

Falluja, or the site where the city now sits, has long been a borderland of sorts: a nexus of peoples, goods and ideas where the ancient north–south and east–west trading routes intersect, and where the various groups from across the wastes converged for business, religious observances and recreation. Today's east–west highway in and out of Iraq still follows the ancient trade route from the Levant through the desert to the multicultural regional hub of Baghdad. One still sees Bedouin families herding their sheep or rolling their big, high-wheeled Mercedes trucks across the open country parallel to the four-lane divided highway.

Falluja is also a city of mosques, almost exclusively Sunni. The population of about 250,000, with another 200,000 living in the city's rural environs, supports scores of mosques large and small. The imams here are respected throughout Sunni Iraq, and their fatwas are regularly sought by people in Baghdad.

When the British invaded Iraq they largely bypassed Falluja: its restive and devout tribesmen were simply not worth the trouble. So the city remained an unofficial capital of warriors, nomads and smugglers who were reluctant to recognize international borders or foreign authorities. Saddam controlled Falluja with a judicious mixture of minimal repression, ample cooptation and steady Baathist resettlement; the town became a popular home for former military and security men. Instead of directly challenging the power of the local clerics and tribal sheikhs, Saddam sought to create bonds of debt and reciprocity by doling out aid and favors in exchange for loyalty or at least compliance. At times he attempted to supplant the established spiritual leaders with younger imams from Baghdad and elsewhere. Amply funded by the government, they would subtly campaign to build pro-Baathist sentiment. Unlike the Shia, who have clear and formal ecclesiastical hierarchies of spiritual and scholarly rank, the Sunni are organized in the more horizontal fashion of a polynucleated scholarly meritocracy, which leaves more room for division and dissension.

Falluja's overlapping and clashing social forces of family, nation, party and faith mean that the city and its sister settlement Ramadi, just down the highway, encapsulate the complex and dangerous politics of Iraq in a particularly concentrated form. For example, the feuds of competing clans overlap and intersect with political conflicts between Islamists, the Baathist old guard, and pro-Coalition sheikhs such as Amir Abderrazzak, head of the provincial council in al-Anbar and his brother, Majed Abderrazzak, who leads a pro-American tribal confederation (interestingly, their father sided with the British in the 1930s).[1] Bisecting all formal politics is the ubiquitous pull of family. Thus, someone might be killed in a political fight, which then sets off a family vendetta. Or conversely, old interfamily hostilities can be articulated through the new war's politics of assassination, snitching and ambush. To get back at a rival, tell the

Americans he is with the resistance. Or tell the resistance that your foe is a US informant.

And now, attempting to control this vortex come the Americans, a people with little sense of history, the world's latest and most unimaginative iteration of empire. Big-boned, well-armed, often well-meaning but almost always totally ignorant of who and what they are dealing with, the Americans are militarily proficient yet political inept. They stumble hopelessly at each crucial juncture. The "Joes" are here on six-month tours; the Marines do yearlong rotations. Their Arabic language skills and cultural knowledge are minimal, while the most important decisions get made in Washington by political advisers with little idea of what is actually happening on the ground.

Between the fall of Baghdad and my visit to the 82nd, five different American commanders have passed through Falluja. All agree that controlling Falluja is "the key" to controlling Iraq, yet none has succeeded in taming the city. In the meantime, al-Anbar province remains one of the very worst places to be a US soldier: IEDs and mortar attacks kill and maim troops with clockwork regularity. In the week before Operation Dozer the guerrillas near Falluja shot down three helicopters.

Relations between the locals and US troops started heading south as soon as the invasion was over. In late April 2003 paratroopers from the 1st Battalion, 325th Regiment of the 82nd Airborne opened fire on a nighttime demonstration against the occupation. The volley cut down scores, leaving thirteen dead and seventy-five wounded, including three young boys. The soldiers say they were attacked by gunmen in the crowd and on rooftops. The protesters insist their rally was peaceful.[2] Things weren't helped by a second incident in which American soldiers killed at least eight Iraqi policemen and a civilian in a gunbattle outside the Jordanian hospital on the edge of town. The shooting happened when a truckload of Iraqi police officers racing through the dark failed to stop for a US checkpoint. Soldiers say the cops fired first.[3] Ryan Martin, a blond and freckled ex-stoner from San Diego who played water polo in community college and then joined the 82nd on a whim, was there. He says that the gunfight was at such close quarters that he ended up blasting away at the back of the police truck with his 9mm pistol. He claims that the dead cops all had Fedayeen tattoos. The truth hardly matters in either of these cases: the people of Falluja hate the US occupation, they hate the US troops, and they are committed to sending the invaders home. From September through March of that first year of occupation Falluja was the responsibility of the 1st Battalion of the 505th of the 82nd. They weren't exactly the same paratroopers who had killed the protesters, but they were close enough as far as the Fallujans were concerned.

To see their counterinsurgency methods up close I decided to "embed" for a while at Forward Operating Base, Camp Volturno. Known informally among the grunts as "Camp Dreamland," the base was once a middle-class resort for government apparatchiks and mid-level Baathist officers. Now its little bungalows are sandbagged barracks while the artificial lake is half-empty, though it is still visited by exotic birds.

I arrived at Dreamland with two filmmakers, Garrett Scott and his easy-going and talented collaborator, Ian Olds. Garrett had returned to Iraq hoping to make a documentary about Howell's squad of Florida National Guardsmen. But when he showed up at the Club, Rodney Sanchez, the much-reviled CO, blew a gasket. Sanchez had not liked an article I'd written about his unit and blamed Garrett for my sins. Garrett in turn blamed me. "He called me a sneak and a liar," said Garrett in a stony rage. As consolation I invited him and Ian to join me in Falluja. In the end, their month-and-a-half-long stay in Iraq's worst hot spot almost got them killed when they just missed an IED blast, but they came away with a film.

Most of our time with the 82nd is spent hanging out, wandering around, talking with soldiers, and watching them watch TV. The squad we are with is run by Sergeant Chris Corcione. Like many Americans of his age and class, Corcione partied hard in his early twenties: he was a small-town metalhead, played in a band, hung out and drove around. He decided to "get in gear" by joining the military. Like many US soldiers, Corcione is a second-generation career soldier. Now he's a staff sergeant leading a squad of eight paratroopers, though he hates jumping out of airplanes. "I force myself to do it every time. It makes me sick." His job in Falluja consists of searching for the elusive resistance, arresting suspected militants and supporters.

When I first meet Corcione he offers me candy. "The reason there's no more candy in the United States—I am sure you've been wondering about this—is because they sent it *all* to Iraq. Have a Jolly Rancher—I insist."

The squad's bungalow is crowded with little cots below which the soldiers keep their personal gear: on homemade plywood shelves along the wall and next to their cots they stash their coffee, fake creamer, sugar, mugs, toothpaste and chewing tobacco. Scattered around are the ubiquitous water bottles half-full of dark tobacco spit. At one end of the room, above Corcione's cot, hangs a huge flag from Ranger School, a Special Forces–style training program for select paratroopers.

Just by the door is a small supply closet that must have been a kitchen or bathroom before Dreamland was looted of all its doors, doorframes, appliances, pipes, wiring, windows, window frames and light fixtures. Now this bare cubicle is stacked with supplies, overflow personal stuff, more candy, guns, body armor and other gear. Near the supply closet hangs a Puerto Rican flag above the bunk of Pfc. Juan Morales, from San Juan by way of Miami. Cattycorner to that, across the room of cots, is Sergeant John Blyler's bunk, above which Old Glory hangs horizontally. Around each bunk the guys have pinned up personal photos, but mostly the walls are covered with neatly clipped and pasted-up pictures of half-naked women, nothing truly pornographic, just the usual busty blondes leering at the camera. As the images crept up toward the ceiling and then onto it the first sergeant, the top noncommissioned officer in the company, decided enough was enough and told the men that they could post no more than three photos each. When the news comes down, Blyler stands on his cot in an angry huff and rips down the images. "Might as well get it over with."

Meanwhile, Sergeant Eric Forbes flips through *People* magazine skimming the recipes. "Well, I'll be damned. You can make a cake out of oranges. Isn't that something?" His flat tone says: *Holy shit, I am in Iraq.* Then looking up at the magazine images of the ladies he begins the tale of how he jilted each one in succession.

"Yeah, she was a nice girl but just not my type. She was also nice, but, I don't know, just not really hot enough." He deadpans, indicating one particularly voluptuous and beautiful model, "She was pretty heartbroken, but ya gotta do what ya gotta do."

"Musta been rough."

"Yeah, you know how it is. She was grabbing my legs begging, 'No, no.'"

A few days later, when everyone is more relaxed, the inevitable necrophilic humor of imperial war-making comes out: "How much money would it take for you to have sex with a male corpse at the fifty-yard line during the Super Bowl halftime show? What? Five million?"

Corcione's squad is part of Alpha Company's 2nd Platoon, which is the responsibility of Matt Bacik, a thoughtful twenty-five-year-old lieutenant and platoon leader, or PL. The IED that killed Sergeant Johnson in downtown Falluja and wounded seven others sent shrapnel into Bacik's buttocks; the hot metal exited across and through his thighs, just missing his testicles.

"I really don't know why my stuff is still there," explains the somewhat bashful Bacik. "The holes just don't line up." After two weeks in the hospital the young officer was back at Volturno, and within a month he was back leading missions.

There are other journalists at Volturno, cycling in and out. And there is also an author. The GIs I meet at the gate bring it up as soon as I arrive. "Yeah, we've got a guy who's an author. He's been here like two months. He's fucking crazy."

"You mean good crazy?"

"No, I mean fucking crazy."

When I first meet Michael Tucker he is marching through the mess hall, bearded and decked out in pale desert camo covered by a long Peshmerga vest. At times like these he would often stop at a table and offer the troops some made-up toast to the war gods and victory and then roll off *Star Wars*–esque aphorisms about the power of "The Force." The GIs would look at him with polite smiles or blank stares and turn back to their Kellogg, Brown & Root–prepared beef stroganoff.

Tucker is also prone to gratuitous use of the word *outstanding*. "Outstanding bunch of guys." "Truly outstanding operation." On missions he wears the usual uniform and helmet, carries a camera and an olive drab satchel on which he's written in black magic marker, "Mike Tucker, Author." On his chest he carries a huge curved gurkha knife with the sharp edge on the inside of the curve. The blade must be ten inches long and four inches at its widest. "The scouts gave it to me up north. Outstanding bunch of guys, very hospitable." Tucker says he is a former Marine and that he has written a book about the Kurds. I found two Mike Tuckers on www.amazon.com; one writes about food, the other about dogs.

Operation Dozer begins in the early morning with the squads all suiting up, donning their Imperator body armor and Kevlar helmets, strapping on the extra ammo for their M-4 rifles, and loading onto the open-bed Humvees. Then we roll out in a long line down to Volturno's south gate. Just before leaving the walls of Volturno the company dismounts and gathers around their bespectacled company commander for one more talking through of the day's mission. The mission is to search houses and bulldoze away guardrails and other obstacles. The CO, Captain Terence Caliguire, is thirty-three years old, short, skinny, an engineer by training—not what you would expect a paratroop captain to look like, but he is smart and his soldiers respect him.

"OK, men. If we're ambushed—get out of the kill zone. All right?" Pause. "What's the kill zone? That's the zone where they try to kill us. So if you're fired on, you keep moving through the zone, then stop, set up a perimeter, and respond. PLs, RTOs," says Caliguire, addressing his platoon leaders and their radio and telephone operators. "Remember: Report, report, report! Gotta let me know what's going on. If you don't report, I don't know." Around him the haze of his breath hangs in the cold morning air. Between sentences he adjusts the tobacco in his lip.

"All right, any questions? Everybody clear on the mission? Any gear broken?" Pause. "Anything anyone needs to tell me?"

Silence.

"All right. Let's go."

From the south gate we roll out to the edge of town in Humvees. To stop bullets and shrapnel the troops have welded thick metal sheets of Armatec plating to the sides of the truck beds, and when that's unavailable they pile up sandbags and hang extra flak vests over the doors. We roll toward Falluja in a cloud of dust. Everyone is tense but calm.

At the edge of Falluja, just before the highway overpass, the famous "cloverleaf," the paratroopers dismount and fan out across the trash-strewn desert looking for IEDs. "Spread out! Keep distance." Then we sweep over the barren embankment of the elevated Highway 10 and down into the north side of town. Once the approach to the town under the highway is secured the Humvees move in, followed by the bulldozer. Off to the east are elements of the 1st Infantry, the Big Red One, and, somewhere on the other edge of town, elements of the 10th Mountain Division. These units have been attached to the 82nd Airborne as part of Task Force Panther.

As Alpha Company searches houses I float between Corcione's squad, Captain Caliguire, and Lt. Bacik. After a morning searching houses and interrogating the locals, Bacik and another platoon leader from Alpha Company move up to "phase line dagger," the next jumping-off point for another "cordon search" of more houses. Lt. Bacik is briefing a superior on his platoon's progress when suddenly we hear two or three loud explosions, someone yells "RPG!" and the air fills with gunfire.

Bacik is running, sprinting as best he can under the weight of a flak vest, ammo and other gear. His young radio operator runs after him. The guns are still snapping away, and the assault is coming from several directions at once. Bacik rounds a corner and heads into some dense side streets to link up with his most forward squad, which is closest to the explosions. A round zings past our heads. I am running a few feet behind Bacik.

"Two-two, move up! Get those trucks out of the alley!" Bacik says, addressing the sergeant in charge of 2nd Squad, 2nd Platoon. We are a block from where the RPGs hit. Word comes in that some of the shots might have originated from an empty school. Bacik and Corcione's squad moves into "search and clear."

As we cross a wide empty lot toward the school, an amplified and fiercely impassioned sermon belts out from the tower of a nearby mosque. If this were a movie the whole thing would reek of cliché: there is almost always some lilting Arabic verse floating in the air like eerie mood music. And now, with this *High Noon*–style walk across the dusty open ground, some unseen imam is yelling wildly in a language few of the paratroopers understand.

"What the fuck is he saying?" someone asks nervously.

"Oh, you know: 'Kill the infidel Americans, they're over there by the school,'" deadpans Corcione. The school is cleared room by room, doors kicked in, locks sawed off, two stories and the roof searched. No RPGs are found, no brass shell casings from AK-47 rounds, and no shooters hiding out. It's back to "phase line dagger" to search more houses.

During these searches the paratroopers are not unduly aggressive, but, as in the school, they often have to damage property, and it is clear that many people, particularly the women and children, are scared. The men are more often humiliated and angry. In most of Iraq, women are not supposed to be seen by strange men. And now the weary paratroopers are rifling through their underwear drawers and herding them outside while their men watch helplessly.

"Who shoots at us from these buildings? Are you with the Baath Party? Hey, get a 'terp over here. Ask this guy if he's with the Baath Party."

As a journalist, even being around these searchers is nauseating, let alone forcing myself to go inside and see or film the action up close. One becomes party to the spectacle of occupation and the ritualized humiliation of the people of Falluja. Even the soldiers, numbed as they are, feel this, and when pressed they will admit it.

"Who are we to search these peoples' homes? Do we really have the right to do this? Yeah, I wonder about that stuff a lot," says Staff Sergeant Luis "Doc" Pacheco, the company medic, one night in his hooch.

During another interview, Staff Sergeant McGuire, who, like the people of Falluja, is deeply religious, puts it quite succinctly: "There's no nice way to search someone's house. I think about how if we did this in eastern Tennessee, where I am from, they'd just as soon shoot you as look at you."

For some of these searches I tag along with an intelligence officer, Captain Mark Zahanczewky, aka Captain Z. His line of questioning keeps returning to the issue of foreign fighters. His subjects keep claiming that the attacks on Americans are the work of Syrians. The intelligence officer seems ideologically predisposed to seeing his work as part of the War on Terrorism and fixates on this theme of bad outsiders. Maybe it's for my benefit. "Ask him if Syrians come here," snaps Z to his interpreter. "Oh, yeah? Look, tell him we got his wife inside, and she says there were Syrians here and that I want to know which one of them is telling the truth."

But when I speak with other soldiers, including Captain Caliguire, they confirm my suspicion that very few foreign fighters have been caught. The reality is that most attacks against US soldiers are the work of locals. When the locals blame Syrians it is a rather transparent attempt to redirect the interest of the US military. What are they going to say? "No, it's us Fallujans who are shooting at you"?

The official line in the military now is: "Everything is intelligence-driven." As one of the war's star generals put it, "You have to be able to identify the structure of who is out there and who their leaders are; what their support system is; where their weapons caches are; who's funding them."[4] If that task is left to monolingual intelligence officers like Captain Z, then put your money on *al-mujahadeen*.

Things on the radio net are getting confused. Because the paratroopers are using a device called Warlock, which jams the radio frequencies used by garage-door openers and other remote-control devices that trigger IEDs, their own radio network is getting scrambled. Bacik's RTO can hear certain parties but not communicate directly with them, so he has to relay messages through other units. In the confusion Bacik is compelled to leave his platoon and walk up to where one of a few tank-like Bradley Fighting Vehicles are guarding the bulldozer's flank. The concern is that the Bradleys are out of touch and could fire on the paratroopers nearby. In fact, Bacik thinks the rounds that just missed us were from a Bradley. Bacik has received orders to tell the Bradleys to change position. As we move forward Bacik stops to explain to Lt. Lipscombe what's going on. It's a quintessential example of stressed-out combat vernacular.

"What's up?" asks Lipscombe.

"The 1st is down there. I gotta tell them to get their fucking crunchy fucking fucknuts the fuck out of there."

"Roger that."

Then it happens again, the rapid *bomb-bomb-bomb* of several RPGs and more small-arms fire. This time an armor-piercing RPG has hit one of the Bradleys; the engine is destroyed, but no one is hurt.

At this point I move forward with Garrett's cinematographer, Ian Olds.

We're creeping down some side streets toward the action, toward the disabled Bradley. On the ground are bits of RPG shrapnel. Along the wall of an abandoned building we see some guys from the 1st Infantry. Just before we head down an alley toward what seems to be the action, we meet Lt. Lipscombe and pause by his Humvee. He's from Delta Company and not a fan of being at war. As he crouches by his Humvee the radio crackles: "Hey, keep an eye out for Tucker."

It seems that Tucker, assigned to the 10th Mountain, has split. He heard the RPGs and shooting and decided to move west looking for the action. Now guys from the Big Red One and 10th Mountain are creeping around trying to find him. But Tucker is around the corner with Bacik and Caliguire and two squads looking for the shooter or shooters. There's more radio traffic about a white car with "bad guys" and an RPG launcher in it circling around. Things are feeling a bit chaotic.

By now I am extremely hungry and drained but wired from the adrenaline. Ian and I have to keep reminding each other to be careful, not to get complacent or too comfortable. Ian has the added task of shooting video, which he does superbly, but at the cost of sometimes becoming dangerously exposed.

"Watch out, man. Your back is sticking around that corner."

"Thanks."

"I don't really feel too scared. Do you?"

"No, not really. And I know that's kinda fucked up."

Then someone is seen dashing across the rooftops of some well-built new two-story homes. He's trapped. The paratroopers storm in and arrest the shooter, a kid of about seventeen. For good measure, they also round up three men in the house from which the kid fired. Bound and soon to be hooded, these guys will eventually end up in the vast and now notorious Abu Ghraib prison, home to almost 13,000 detainees, a subset

of more than 40,000 that the Coalition has taken. Right now they are being interrogated. Then inside the house there's a commotion.

"What the fuck are you looking at?! Don't fucking look at me, *bitch!*
Don't look at me, bitch! We'll send your fucking ass to Cuba!"

It's Tucker, gurkha knife drawn. He's losing it, flipping out on a young
man who is bound and sitting in the house. Mike Tucker, author, on vacation in Iraq, is threatening "Haji" with a huge knife. Mike Tucker, late forties, white, former soldier, maybe a writer, is joy-riding with the legion-
naires. This is war as extreme tourism or high-stakes role-playing game.
It is the Conradian end of the river where empire's lawless opportunities
mix with personal madness to form a potent political and psychedelic
cocktail. But it is almost as if Tucker is invading the war movies running
in all our heads. Ian and Garrett don't film the outburst because it is just
too weird. The soldiers, who are also constantly documenting their own
adventures with digital cameras, seem equally disconcerted. *Is he really
part of the script?* Oh yes, he is. The scene doesn't last long.

"All right, fuck this!" snaps Captain Z. He wants the suspects zip-tied,
bagged and hauled out to the trucks. "Get these fucking guys outta here.
Take 'em all. I want 'em all in the fucking trucks."

Now it's really late and the shadows are growing long. Several IEDs
have been found and destroyed in huge controlled blasts. The longer we
stay in town the more time the resistance has to set up attacks. Ian and I
pull back to where most of the paratroopers are staging to leave Falluja.
Their trucks line the main road in an orderly "herringbone" formation.

As the coffle of prisoners is brought forward on a Humvee, then unloaded and marched to another, Tucker brings up the rear, bearded mug
in a mean grimace, his gurkha knife raised straight above his head in a
victory salute to the war gods. Later, Tucker spots me, his fellow writer,
as I am moving along the line of Humvee trucks trying to find Bacik and

figure out what's going on. From about fifty yards away he stands up in the back of a Humvee, arm in the air, gurkha knife to the sky and hails me with a roar.

"*Jedi warrior!*"

I pretend not to hear.

The trucks move out in slow, orderly stages, then make a high-speed dash under the cloverleaf and down the dusty stretch of road back to the safety of FOB Volturno, where the only risks are occasional mortar rounds.

During Operation Dozer's after-action report the issues discussed are all tactical. Alpha Company's commander, the very serious and bespectacled Captain Caliguire, runs down the list of what worked and what didn't. Absent from the discussion is the issue of winning hearts and minds. "On that front," explains Caliguire later, "we do our best. We treat people with respect and dignity, but you can't win them all. Security comes first. Do people resent the house searches? Yes. But my job is to bring security to Falluja and keep my men safe. And there's not gonna be any reconstruction or NGOs or UN in here if there isn't security first."

Relaxing on his cot, Lt. Bacik makes similar points. "I do what I am told. If they want me to build a bridge, I'll do it. But right now we have to suppress this resistance. We fight with restraint and discipline and concern for civilians, but this is a war."

In short, the 82nd is focusing on what seems to work best—"search and attack." That means arresting and killing the underground and its supporters. The methods in this fight are cordon search operations, undercover Special Forces, local spies and information extracted from detainees—who, by the Pentagon's own admission, are subject to effective psychological torture such as isolation and prolonged sleep deprivation. Using whatever intelligence it can get, the 82nd launches continuous lightning raids in and out of Falluja. As for the delicate task of winning the people's loyalty, that will have to be someone else's job—someone who can provide work, fix the electricity, clean up the garbage and get Iraq's oil flowing. In the meantime, the war in Falluja is far from over.

What do the troops think of all this? Bacik, a West Point grad, twenty-five, and very good at what he does, stays on message, stays positive, and is circumspect about his doubts. Lt. Lipscombe, who I meet first at a big operational briefing and then later when his platoon from Delta Company is holding down some streets in Falluja, is immediately more candid: "I am not sure I want to stay in the military. I've got a little baby I haven't seen." But opting to not re-enlist (one of the main ways disaffection with the war is expressed) is a no-no in the culture of the professional military. The career NCOs cajole, then threaten and ridicule and emotionally ice-out soldiers who don't sign re-enlistment papers. Doc Pacheco is getting a taste of the re-enlistment pressure. The grunts call this campaign of harassment "getting the panther penis" because they are part of Task Force Panther; sometimes it's just called "the 82 inches."

Pacheco is a valuable asset: muscled, tough, fit, he's a combat medic with advanced skills, and at the young age of twenty-three he could be good for at least a decade more of jumping out of airplanes, shooting at bad guys and clamping shut ripped-open arteries. But Pocheco doesn't want to be a career soldier; he joined the military as a way to become a Chicago firefighter.

"The best way to get into the department is as an EMT. But those classes are really expensive. If you join the army they pay for it." Pocheco has done his time, which included cleaning up the brains of a friend who was shot in a accidental discharge in Afghanistan. Pacheco wants out.

"When they try to get you to re-enlist, they always say, 'What are you gonna do out there? You'll be sucking dick for beer money.' That's one of the first sergeant's favorite lines," says Pacheco, sitting on the edge of his cot and jiggling his legs nervously. His bunkmates joke grimly about the military and how they are trying to screw Pacheco. But the doc, fresh from a hot trip to Falluja, wears the expression of a hurt boy.

"I think I did my part. I never wanted to stay in the military my whole life. I think they should accept that and stop fucking with me."

Along with the glares and verbal abuse from the NCOs, the Green Machine's faceless bureaucracy is also pushing "the panther penis" by losing Pacheco's pay records, deleting his accumulated vacation time and making the ensuing appeal process a nightmare of red tape.

Other soldiers seem less affected by the pressure. Ryan Martin, the water polo player, is oblivious to the pressure. Like many guys in this company Martin also served in Afghanistan.

"Those recruiting posters? Man, the cooler that shit looks the more it sucks!" says Martin. As he rails away, a meek lieutenant from the mortar platoon walks by, Bible in hand, headed to Sunday chapel, pretending not to hear the rant. "Crawling through swamps. Sleeping in the mud, putting paint on your face —all that Special Forces shit? I've done all that—it *fucking sucks!* I tell all my friends—those ads, right?—the cooler that shit looks the more it *fucking sucks ass!*"

One of Ryan's buddies is Joseph Wood, the company armorer and a roommate of Doc Pacheco. He's boyishly handsome, with a mother from Venezuela, the land of beauty queens, while his father is a dissolute, downwardly mobile southern aristocrat. Above his bunk hang Tibetan prayer flags, he burns incense, wears flip-flops around, and reads books about spirituality. He served in Afghanistan, jumping out of choppers and pulling security for teams of Special Forces operatives. Now he wants to move to New York and design women's clothing. He already has a stunningly crafted portfolio. So single-minded is Wood in his quest for an art education and a career that the army's re-enlistment pressures are irrelevant to him. "Man, the army is for fucking zombies, people who can't think for themselves." And he's antiwar, but in a weird, frontline combat sort of way.

"I don't think we should be here—it's all about oil. But I am not a pacifist. Anyone fucks with us, we'll light 'em up. They gotta understand that." At another time he tells me: "The army sucks, but I am not saying people shouldn't join. I mean, the army can be cool; it's about defending our freedoms. Know what I mean?"

"No, not sure I follow."

Generally there is not much political discourse at Dreamland. The military inculcates a decidedly apolitical culture. The soldier's job is to serve and follow orders. They are free to believe anything or nothing at all as long as they serve America.

I corner Lt. Bacik in the gear-crowded hut of the platoon squad to ask him about politics and the war.

"American soldiers can *feel* however they want. If they don't like Iraqis, that's their right. We're all free-thinking Americans," says Bacik. "But they have to listen to what their leadership says. They have to obey orders. Soldiers don't have to like what they do—they just have to do it." This ethos creates a political culture of relative quiet, though GIs will express doubts and at times profound confusion. Pacheco in particular seemed to really struggle. "I really wonder what this is all about. I really do."

Talking to these young soldiers I begin to feel that many of them didn't have the skills to answer their own questions. They have satellite TV and Internet access, but putting the bits and pieces together—some BBC here, a critical article from the Net there—is a rare thing on most military bases. Usually, the war is framed as patriotic duty or through the narrative of private personal trauma.

Eventually Falluja would come to look like the beginning of the end for the American project in Iraq. Consider the state of reconstruction in al-Anbar province. The occupodians and their colleagues at Halliburton were largely useless in improving or repairing services and providing jobs. The army did what it could on its own. Taking a page from the domestic war on drugs, the military allowed its frontline commanders to use seized cash for local reconstruction; this was called the Commanders' Emergency Assistance Program or CEAP. But by November these funds were mostly gone, and the army's small-scale potable water and garbage clearance programs began to go broke. In some places, like Baquba, not even the Iraqi police were getting paid.

In Falluja the 82nd Airborne tackled reconstruction in a particularly impotent fashion. For lack of money, the 82nd turned to the infinitely abundant ether of the Internet and set up a website called "Falluja Works."

"The website allows building contractors or merchants to link up with potential customers, like homeowners or other businesses," explains Dreamland's CO, the grinning Lt. Col. Drinkwine, during an interview in front of Garrett's cameras. Drinkwine is sitting in a plastic chair, looking pudgy and pale, spouting one gung-ho platitude after another. "Falluja is a tough town. But it's a great place for young soldiers. We're a steely-eyed bunch. I say, if you want a challenge, if you want to be productive, join the army. Join the infantry. Come to Falluja."

The absurdity of Drinkwine's website scheme is amplified by its supreme condescension. Falluja, ancient Bedouin trading center, a city at war lacking a functioning phone system or steady electricity, is offered a website to kick-start its economic recovery.

"Falluja Works" is emblematic of bad US military thinking. Though many US officers are very bright and well educated, the vast majority of those I met held engineering or chemistry degrees. They tended to approach problems in a mechanical or purely tactical fashion. Few had degrees or had even taken classes in history, psychology or anthropology. Cultural intuition was not their strong suit.

Shortly after I left Camp Dreamland there occurred a rather spectacular assault. On February 14 more than forty insurgents launched a multipronged attack on the police station in the heart of the city while other insurgents pinned down the Iraqi Civil Defense force and provided blocking measures that included at least three attacks on the 82nd. AP described the attack as follows: "Guerrillas shouting 'God is great' launched a bold daylight assault ... meeting little resistance as they gunned down policemen and freed prisoners in a battle that killed 23 people ..."

The 82nd Airborne's press release described the day as follows, mentioning the assault as if it were unrelated to a blocking maneuver against its Quick Reaction Force or QRF:

> During the morning of Feb. 14 in Fallujah, 30 to 35 enemy personnel conducted an attack on the Iraqi Police station and Iraqi Civil Defense Corps Headquarters. The attacks killed 23 Iraqi policemen and wounded 30 other people while the ICDC had no casualties. Enemy forces conducted a supporting attack against the ICDC headquarters while they conducted the main attack against the police station, freeing 72 prisoners.
>
> At approximately 9 a.m. Feb. 14, paratroopers were attacked by rocket-propelled grenades and small arms fire. Coalition forces suffered one US wounded in action from the engagement, but his wounds were not life threatening.

At approximately 11:15 a.m. Feb. 14 in 3rd Brigade's area of operations, paratroopers were conducting a combat patrol when they were attacked with an improvised explosive device north of Lutafiyah. The blast wounded one soldier.[5]

Garrett and Ian were at Dreamland that day, waiting at the gate for a ride back to Baghdad, when they heard the shooting. We had all met some of the guys from the company that sent the QRF, which got ambushed at the cloverleaf. One GI we had met at the gate on our first day was very badly wounded and shipped to Germany for treatment.

In Baghdad, the Coalition's dissemblers tried to implicate al-Qaeda in the Falluja attack, hoping that this could give the occupation legitimacy as part of the global War on Terror. But then came glimpses of the truth: US forces arrested the mayor of Falluja. He was one of eight local officials who quit a day after the bloody guerrilla raid in the town. And there were rumors that the two insurgents who were captured alive were members of the ICDC.

After that attack, Muhammad's Army, which US officials say appears to be an umbrella group for former Iraqi intelligence agents and army officers, distributed pamphlets warning Iraqis who collaborated with the Americans to prepare for harsh consequences. Before long I got an e-mail from Joseph Wood:

Hey in other news, some crazyness has been going on w/ some of our interpreters and contractors getting shot up by locals. The other day, Sammy (one of the guys who drives around Dreamland in a van, selling shit) was driving to Baghdad w/ one of our interpreters, and some dudes pulled them over to the side of the road and shot them. The interpreter was killed and Sammy is in ICU. A few days earlier, the Chicken Man (another guy who sells shit on Dreamland) got whacked also. Pretty crazy huh?

By March the army was handing Dreamland over to the Marine 1st Expeditionary Force. The Marines had criticized the army's methods in Falluja as weak. Through some unspecified combination of better tactics the Marines were going to tame the city. They sent in a big foot patrol, which got attacked. Then the four mercenaries from Blackwater Inc. were ambushed, and their bodies were burnt, dragged through the streets, and hung from a bridge.

As revenge, the Marines laid siege to the city for almost a month. During that time some friends of mine, Dahr Jamail, Jo Wilding and David Martinez, went into Falluja. They saw a city in rebellion with hundreds of civilians killed and wounded. At one point Jo and David were riding in an ambulance that was fired on by Marine snipers. Soon the Marines were bombing mosques in Falluja. Marine Lieutenant Colonel Brennan Byrne, looking dazed and disassociated, told the BBC: "We always win. We're the Marines."

Meanwhile, in Fort Bragg, Bacik, Corcione, Pacheco and the rest of the guys from the 1st of the 505th downshifted to half-days on duty, meals at Outback Steakhouse and the freedom of rolling in their own private automobiles. The Reuters financial wire brought the following:

New York, April 7. COMEX gold prices reversed course and moved into positive territory Wednesday morning after reports said an Iraqi mosque had been shelled and 40 people killed, traders said. COMEX silver trimmed substantial losses on the reports.

Gold added to gains when Reuters reported witnesses saying the office of a religious organization near the mosque in Falluja was hit by a rocket during heavy fighting between US troops and guerrillas. They said there were a number of casualties.

"Gold's popping up on that news, and silver popped up. We're reacting to this thing. We're rallying on this thing," said one COMEX floor broker.[6]

Not a month before, proconsul Bremer had told the press that the local resistance was beaten or mostly finished; all that remained were some foreign "jihadists." By the end of April the Marines had called off their siege and given Falluja over to a new militia of former Baathist soldiers called the Falluja Protection Army. When Dahr Jamail went back into Falluja on May 10 he saw the FPA and the Iraqi police fraternizing with the armed *mujahadeen*. The locals consider their city liberated. On world markets oil climbed toward $40 a barrel as speculators finally started to worry about the adventure in Iraq.

8

Land of the Lost

> The Christian in me says it's wrong, but the corrections officer in me
> says, "I love to make a grown man piss himself."
>
> Abu Ghraib guard Spc. Charles Graner,
> as quoted by Spc. Joseph M. Darby

The true nature of Operation Iraqi Freedom appears most clearly
in its capricious use of mass detention. It is in this regard that the
American occupation most resembles the regime it replaced.

Abu Ghraib, Iraq's largest prison, sits just east of Baghdad. From the
highway it offers only the sterile view of a long cement wall punctuated
by guard towers. The wall runs parallel to the Amman–Baghdad road
for roughly three-quarters of a mile, but it seems farther. Inside Abu
Ghraib as many as 15,000 detainees at any one time are held in large,
open-air camps: tents surrounded by razor wire and watched over by
armed guards—an Iraqi Andersonville. In February 2004 a confidential
Red Cross report quoted an American military intelligence officer as es-
timating that between 70 and 90 percent of all Iraqi prisoners had been
arrested "by mistake."

Months before the infamous torture photos hit the news I make my way to Abu Ghraib on a bright sunny day, accompanying a young woman from Adamiya named Zainab who is looking for her father and brother. They had been arrested during a house search conducted by the 124th Infantry—the same unit that includes Howell's squad.

The raid was typical: bad intel, wrong address, no weapons, the family (originally sympathetic to the US) gets busted anyway. Zainab speaks English and works at an Internet café. She wears stylish clothes and a cream-colored *hejab* that makes her face look puffy and stressed. She has a girlish manner but at the same time exudes a cool, disassociated confidence, a sense of mission. At a restaurant, Zainab, accompanied by a male friend, explains how her relatives were arrested: "One of the soldiers tried to pull off my headscarf and I screamed. My father tried to stop the soldier and they just arrested him. And when my brother complained they arrested him, too."

After the bust, Zainab worked up her courage and went to the Club—the base where I had embedded—and confronted the soldiers at the gate. "I was very angry," she says. "I yelled and screamed at them for my father. I think the soldiers became scared of me." Finally, the Florida Guardsmen relented to Zainab's yelling and brought down an officer, who looked into the matter. Zainab's father and brother had already been sent to Abu Ghraib, charged with assaulting US soldiers.

Since the raid, Zainab's mother has become sick and depressed; she's been having strange stress-related seizures. She's an older woman, middle class, and has lived her entire adult life with Zainab's father. Now he is lost in the bowels of a huge detention camp. The responsibility of earning money and getting the men out of prison has fallen to Zainab. She copes with the stress by taking Valium. "So I can sleep," she giggles.

Zainab has a contact of sorts at the prison: a lecherous Iraqi translator. "He says if I marry him he will let me see my father." She has no plans to marry the collaborator or to perform any sexual favors for him, but she's trying to play him while he does the same to her. "I think he will let me in if I just act like I will marry him."

Zainab, Akeel and I head out to the prison in an old Mercedes cab. Zainab will try to get some medicine to her father. She says that the sleazy translator has offered to free her father for $15,000. "I think I can get him down to $3,000," says Zainab. "Anyway, that is all we have."

In front of Abu Ghraib there are always small crowds of people trying to find their relatives. To even speak with soldiers or translators at the front gate, visitors must wait in a line that snakes through a gravel-filled lot divided by a maze of Jersey barriers topped with razor wire. Above the scene rises a cement gun tower, its windows blocked with sandbags. To be in line is to be in a pen, watched over by soldiers. GIs occasionally emerge from the tower to yell at the civilians who approach the front gate without joining the immobile line.

"Move! Get back! Move!" No one on the ground understands. One man asks Akeel if the soldiers are yelling insults.

While Zainab liaises with the creepy translator (I ask if I can be of assistance but she declines), Akeel and I do interviews and surreptitiously snap photos, both of which are prohibited outside Abu Ghraib. One journalist I know was booted out of the parking lot by MPs as soon as he arrived; another, a woman, was attacked by the crowd but quickly escaped.

The people milling about in front of the prison include some former detainees who have returned to help their friends and family inside. One such man is Harb Muhammad, a farmer from Tikrit who had been arrested and detained with eight of his male relatives. After almost six months he was released, but his kin are still locked away.

"I was accused of being the eyes for the resistance, watching the military while I worked my fields," Muhammad explains. "First I was held near Tikrit and interrogated." But after about a week he and his relatives were shipped to Abu Ghraib, on August 5, 2003, and never again questioned. Once in Abu Ghraib Muhammad languished in an open-air camp, growing a beard and wearing a filthy prison jumpsuit. He waited for months without explanation. Then one day in December "they came with a truck and just told me to get in. And over by the market they told us to get out," he says, pointing toward Abu Ghraib village on the other side of the prison. "They still have eight of my relatives in there. I have to help them. If they have no future, I have no future."

"There are fathers in there with their sons who are as young as thirteen. There are lots of teenagers," says Muhammad. "At one point our family got a lawyer, but he just took our money and left. There is no law here. Even 90 percent of the soldiers say they know you are innocent but they can do nothing to let you go. It is very bad, there is not enough food, not enough water and many people are sick inside. During Eid, at the end of Ramadan, we had a big demonstration in some of the camps. We shouted 'Allahu Akbar!' Some people threw stones and the soldiers started shooting. I heard that they injured twenty people, but I only saw one man shot in the hand."

During the interview we try to be inconspicuous, crouching on the gravel behind a berm and some blast barriers. Muhammad says that he saw three different demonstrations by prisoners during his detention. The protests in response to bad conditions were met with more abuse. "The soldiers do very bad things. They step on the food to make it dirty." He and other men who are standing nearby tell stories of frequent psychological torture—mostly sleep deprivation, lack of adequate food, limited water—and widespread illness and bureaucratic chaos. "There is no process, no lawyers. They just put you in a tent and forget about you."

I ask about Sunni–Shia relations. "There is no division. We are all united. We are all Muslims and we all hate the Americans." At this point another former detainee joins in. His name is Hajl Sabor, and he shows me some discharge papers with a serial number. He says he was in Camp Six inside Abu Ghraib. With Akeel translating, he says, "Look, I have a message for George Bush. Tell him he is an asshole. But also, I thank George Bush because now we are all brothers—Shia and Sunni together."

What does he think should be done? "Solution?" says Haji Sabor. "They take mothers away from their little children. This is an affront to Islam. They are awful. There is no solution, there is no formal way out of this, there is only *al-jihad!*"

I check with Akeel as to what exactly Sabor means by this. "He means *jihad*. Holy war, not just struggle in the path of God," explains Akeel with a look that says, *Silly journalist, what do you think is going on here? Jihad* is not the answer one usually gets in Iraq. More often one finds a complex and contradictory, sometimes unrealistic set of suggestions that come down to: Leave our oil alone and get the UN in to supervise elections so we can have an Islamic government. What exactly that last point means is interpreted in a whole spectrum of ways. But rarely do Iraqis—who have been through two decades of constant fighting—suggest more war. Other men join the conversation with more stories.

"They smashed everything in my house because I was a member of the Baath Party," says one man. "They capture lots of students, they are afraid of the Iraqi students," says another. One man calmly pushes closer while the others are getting riled up and talking with each other. "Write this down: They shot a man in the chest. His name was Mazan Thuwany Daud, number 152615. He was shot in the chest and they took him away. I do not know if he lived. I am not lying. Write it down."

Our little throng isn't so little or quiet any more and has attracted the attention of some MPs in a Humvee. They pull up on the other side of the wire-topped berm. One of the MPs gets out and swaggers up and down, his helmet and body armor stiffening his gait, a huge unlit cigar jammed in the side of his mouth, hatred radiating through his wraparound mir-rored shades. He is such a cliché that I recall feeling disappointment and thinking, "Too bad no one will actually believe how ridiculous this guy is when I try to describe him."

In the near distance are three loud explosions, too big to be mortars. Everyone's attention is drawn to the horizon. The throng disperses and the swaggering GI gets back in his Humvee and takes off.

After several more trips to Abu Ghraib, Zainab gets to see her father and brother. They confirm the general story: bad food, abuse, lack of water, no due process. "My father says they have half of Falluja in there," says Zainab after her visit. I do not ask Zainab what sort of deal she has worked out with the Iraqi translator.

The lobby of the Swan Lake Hotel has the decor of a Chinese restaurant: the walls are dark; the couches and lounge chairs are of the overstuffed, slightly fuzzy red and purple variety. Garish vases hold barren twig arrangements. To one side is the hotel bar, but no alcohol is served, only tea. The Swan Lake, with its big white English-language sign out front, is Al-Jazeera's Baghdad bureau; many of the staff live and work upstairs.

I am having tea with Salah Hassan, a haggard and sad-looking Al-Jazeera cameraman. He is thirty-two years old, the father of two young children, and he is telling me about being tortured by American soldiers in Abu Ghraib. It's late January 2004, and the photo revelations of tor-ture at the hands of Lynndie England, Charles Graner and the rest of that demented night shift are still months away. As Salah unwinds his tale

I worry that my editors in New York might not believe him. (To their credit, they do.)

Salah Hassan explains how on November 3 of last year he raced to the site of a roadside bomb attack on a US military convoy in Dialla, near the eastern Iraqi city of Baquba. While he was interviewing people at the scene, US troops who had previously taken photographs of Hassan at other events arrested him, took him to a police station, interrogated him, and repeatedly accused him of knowing in advance about the bomb attack and of lying in wait to get video footage.

"I told them to review my tapes, that it was clear I had arrived thirty or forty minutes after the blast. They told me I was a liar," says Hassan.

From Baquba Hassan was taken to the military base at Baghdad International Airport, held in a bathroom for two days, then flown hooded and bound to Tikrit. After two more days in another bathroom, he was loaded onto a five-truck convoy of detainees and shipped south to Abu Ghraib.

Once inside the sprawling prison Hassan says he was greeted by US soldiers who sang "Happy Birthday" to him through his tight plastic hood, stripped him naked and addressed him only as "Al-Jazeera," "boy" or "bitch." He was forced to stand hooded, bound and naked for eleven hours in the bitter autumn night air; when he fell, soldiers kicked his legs to get him up again. In the morning, he was made to wear a dirty red jumpsuit that was covered with someone else's fresh vomit and was then interrogated by two Americans in civilian clothes—perhaps one of the infamous Tiger Teams contracted from CACI International with linguists from Titan Inc. They made the usual accusations that Hassan and Al-Jazeera were in cahoots with "terrorists."

While most Abu Ghraib prisoners are held in large, barrack-like tents in open-air compounds surrounded by razor wire, Hassan says he was locked in a high-security isolation unit of tiny cells. Down the tier from him was an old woman who sobbed incessantly and a mentally deranged thirteen-year-old girl who would scream and shriek until the American guards released her into the hall, where she would run up and down; exhausted, she would eventually return to her cell voluntarily. Hassan says that all the other prisoners in the unit, mostly men, were ordered to remain silent or risk being punished with denial of food, water and light.

Elsewhere in Abu Ghraib, Hassan's colleague Suheib Badr Darwish was also in lockup. He had been arrested in Samarra on November 18 and, according to a colleague of his at Al-Jazeera, was badly beaten by US troops.

Meanwhile, on the outside, the network hired a topflight lawyer named Hider Nur al-Mulha to start working Hassan's case through Iraq's largely wrecked court system. Eventually Hassan was brought before a panel of the Iraqi Governing Council's freshly minted Supreme Court, which was set up alongside its War Crimes Tribunal for trying the likes of Saddam Hussein and his henchmen. The case of Salah Hassan, journalist, was the court's first. He was released for lack of evidence against him. After three more days in Abu Ghraib, this time held in one of the prison's open-air camps, Hassan, still in his vomit-stained red jumpsuit, was dumped on a street just outside Baghdad on December 18. Darwish was released more than a month later on January 25, again for lack of incriminating evidence.

M ass incarceration is only a subset of a larger logic: collective punishment of civilians as counterinsurgency. It is a strategy, or set of tactics, born of political failure and desperation.

In Samarra, I meet the newly arrived Stryker Brigade, named after the unit's special new armored personnel carriers, which have high wheels and elaborate medieval-looking metal grilles skirting their sides. The cage-like grilles are designed to catch and thus minimize the blast impact of RPGs. Attila, Dahr and I drove up to Samarra through Operation Ivy Blizzard because Attila had heard reports of house demolitions. On the way up we saw US troops burning brush along the roadside, cutting down trees and sweeping the villages.

They've been only three weeks "in country" and the Strykers have already lost five guys and two vehicles. One of the nervous GIs, in the middle of a big cordon search operation, confirms what some local men told us: not far away the resistance knocked out a Stryker with a mine. In response, the Stryker Brigade destroyed two homes with bulldozers. Kiowa choppers circle low overhead looking for snipers while the soldiers search homes and interrogate suspects.

A female civil affairs officer approaches us. She gives me her father's phone number. "Can you call him? Tell him I am OK. We haven't had any e-mail or mail or phone calls since we got here." She seems dazed and profoundly freaked out.

Near Balad, there is more of the same. The village of Abu Hishma, a hamlet of 7,000 on a flat plain above a wide bend in the Tigris near where I met the rural resistance cell, is on lockdown.

After a series of resistance attacks, one of which killed a GI, the local US commander, Lt. Colonel Nathan Sassaman, scaled the village with triple coils of razor wire and threatened to deport the residents to a resettlement camp further east if the violence continued. Now the people of Abu Hishma carry special identification cards and must abide by a dawn-to-dusk curfew. There is only one way in and out of town, which passes through a police-controlled checkpoint. On top of that, Colonel Sassaman has forced 126 community leaders, family sheikhs and less powerful *moktars,* to sign a contract promising that each signatory will submit to incarceration if there is any resistance activity in their areas of responsibility. It's a form of institutional hostage-taking and it makes perfect sense—in a vicious, colonial sort of way.

At the village gate the mood is one of defeat. "They treat us like Palestinians," complains a farmer, then in English adds: "Sassaman—Ariel Sharon number one." Several Iraqi police are standing nearby playing with their Kalashnikov rifles, but instead of trying to shut down the criticism, they join in. "They treat us like dirt. We just take orders from the Americans. The whole thing is ridiculous." Then breaking into laughter one cop adds, "Our chief of police is in jail in Balad right now!"

Saddam's hometown of Awja, further north near Tikrit, is also surrounded by wire. Since the triple layer of shiny sharp coils went up and the residents started carrying new IDs, guerrilla activity in this area has dropped off dramatically.

"Any Haji comes near the wire, we shoot 'em. One of our scouts has like fifty-five confirmed kills," claims Spc. Keltner, a soldier with the 22nd Infantry who is guarding the checkpoint at the village entrance. Inside Awja all is quiet. The few people around seem meek and resigned, but as we leave the troops at the gate uncover a cache of RPGs. "Fucking Mortar Man!" says a GI, referring to a lone resistance fighter who still plagues them. "This was right on the other side of the berm. They were gonna hit the guard shack." We snap some photos and leave before Mortar Man makes his next move.

On the southern edge of Baghdad, under a date palm canopy and among the misty winter fields of al-Doura, there is more evidence of collective punishment, the logic of detention on a national scale.

A day ago an IED took out an American Humvee. The road where the bomb struck is littered with debris and a few bloody military-issued handages, but the Humvee has been carted off. In retaliation, the local US forces spent the night dropping mortar rounds on nearby farms.

A man named Abdel gives us a tour of his crop beds. Poking up from the brown stalks are between fifteen and twenty clean, white unexploded US mortar rounds. Another farmer from the area claimed that the military said it would remove the explosives only when the farmers handed over resistance fighters. Abdel is furious: "How I am going to plant my crops?"

As he laments the situation a gaggle of young boys who have followed us to the field start throwing rocks at the mortar rounds. The explosives are all around us. I am with Ian Olds on this outing, and we've both been taking closeup photos and shooting video: we are well within the potential blast range.

"Hey! Whoa! Whoa! Stop! What *the fuck* are they doing!"

I can't believe my eyes. An older boy yells at the kids to stop, and Abdel gives them a quick scolding. We move away from the unexploded rounds and then Abdel very formally resumes his comments right where he had left off.

In the distance a brace of Black Hawk copters races toward us, skimming low across the treetops so that gunmen on the ground have less time to aim. Their rotors beat with an ominous clatter: the pulse of war.

9

Subjects of the New Regime

The new State of Iraq owes to the British Royal Air Force a debt bigger than it can ever repay. For it was the work of the Air Force which more than anything else enabled the League of Nations in 1932 to decide that Iraq was fit for independence.

Ernst Main, *Iraq: From Mandate to Independence*, 1935

The sky above Ramadi is heavy with brown dust; gusts of wind bend the reeds along the road, the palms sway erratically. Akeel, Rob and I have come here to find one of the town's leading sheikhs.

Al-Ramadi, a city of about 400,000, is the capital of al-Anbar province and lies along the Euphrates only about an hour and a half west of Baghdad. The city seems untouched by the Green Zone's occupodian fantasies. Some nine months after the conquest Ramadi still suffers water shortages and long blackouts. The local population of farmers, merchants, state sector–oriented building contractors and clerics is angry, and the resistance here is strong. The vibe is one of constant danger; Western reporters tend to steer clear of Ramadi—though there are exceptions, like the superb Patrick Graham, who lived here for a while. Even Akeel, Mr. Bravado himself, is on his best behavior. With the sheikh's blessings we hope to travel around Ramadi and its environs in relative safety so we can interview civilians about life under US occupation.

On our first trip to find the sheikh the resistance kills two French contractors and we get caught in the ensuing traffic jam. Akeel's buddy Hassan, a taciturn shopkeeper from Adhamiya, is at the wheel of his minivan. We are playing a musical driving game that Iraqis call "this is your fate." With the car radio on someone will announce, "The next song is your fate!" and name someone else in the car. Whatever music follows is deciphered for its metaphorical meanings.

Akeel gets the first tune, a cloying globo-pop love song—perfect, since his future wife is psychologically torturing him by running hot, then cold, then hot. Eshelman is next with a bad cover of "American Woman," which fits since he is hooking up with a cute British lady and an American aid worker he had been flirting with had just cracked one of his ribs in a playful wrestling match. (The words of the song, you will recall, are "American woman—stay away from me.") I get the James Bond theme song. Then just before Hassan's turn he says, "Watch, it'll be the weather."

Instead, we hit traffic, never a good sign after dark in the middle of the Iraqi desert. Soon, cars in front of us are cutting across the scrubland alongside the highway, their headlight beams bouncing through the columns of dust. Ahead on the road, soldiers are conducting some sort of sweep, occasionally popping illumination flares into the sky: the brilliant incandescence floats down on small parachutes to reveal a quick, five- or six-second snapshot of the scene below. Somewhere farther on are the two dead contractors.

"Now you see more of the traffic freedom. Isn't it really great? I feel so lucky that you Americans came to my country," says Akeel as we bounce into the desert past the US soldiers. Heading out the next day, Rob is somewhat testy.

"They whacked two honkies on this road yesterday and we're right behind them. Let's just say I am a little bit edgy, OK?"

Eshelman is rarely nervous. A former housing activist, street-fighting Berlin squatter and more recently the chief aide to San Francisco's president of the Board of Supervisors, Rob generally stays pretty cool. A punk-rock, working-class autodidact with a masochistic streak, Rob has recently been reporting from the West Bank. In San Francisco I had seen him pick fights with guys much bigger than himself. One such incident ended with Rob's leg in a cast (after that we gave him a little trophy of a boxer with an engraved inscription reading "bone crusha"). He was also the first American to do prison time in the Czech Republic. There was a misunderstanding that ended with Rob serving several months on misplaced charges of attempted auto theft. He lived in a cell full of illegal Russian immigrants, playing cards and getting time in the yard only once a week. For him to be nervous about the trip to Ramadi is not good.

When we finally arrive, Akeel has to stop for smokes. Waiting on the street for him we hear a loud, close bang. A speeding pickup truck has just bottomed out in a rut a few yards away. It tears past at lighting speed, then the driver slams on the brakes and takes a sharp left a few blocks down. In the truck's bed is an *Ali Babba* or resistance fighter, an *aqal* headscarf wrapped around his face, a Kalashnikov in one hand while the other hand grips the side of the vehicle for dear life. In hot pursuit comes a police car, both officers waving guns out the window.

"Welcome to Ramadi," says Rob with a mock grin. We drive all over town and see no American patrols.

Muhammad Mahmoud Letief is a leading religious sheikh in Ramadi. He's a member of the powerful Duleimi clan. Tall and regal, he wears a long gray *dishadasha* and the red-checked *aqal* common among the al-Anbar tribes. Only thirty-eight years old, the sheikh is already a venerated scholar and mediator with a PhD in religious studies. He is president of the religious sanctum of Anbar, a community of scholars associated with the Ramadi's main mosque, and he is president of the Department of Koranic Studies at Anbar College.

As a religious "sheikh" or "leader," Dr. Letief's status is scholarly and ecclesiastic. He is not a tribal sheikh; his status does not flow simply from holding a place of prominence in a powerful and politically connected family. Nor is his status the product of being rich or good at business. In fact, his home is surprisingly modest.

The majority of people in al-Anbar, regardless of their occupation, are still connected to the old rhythms of the desert or the agriculture villages along the Euphrates, which bends through here. Like Falluja, Ramadi is an old trading center, very religious with complicated local politics. It is one of those backwaters, like rural Maine, or parts of the US South, that for insiders feels like the center of a universe, distinct and better than those soft places outside and beyond. But to a visitor Ramadi feels isolated. The sheikh bears all the local Bedouin pride but also exudes a worldliness and intellectual sophistication that clashes with the dusty provincialism of Ramadi's sand-colored homes and quiet streets.

On the way in Akeel had turned around from the front passenger seat of Hassan's van and explained, "With a guy like this, you don't really ask many questions. It's more about letting him talk and just listening."

When we meet Sheikh Letief the second time he ushers us into his *diwan* and introduces us to his brother and a cousin. Then he begins to explain the situation: sporadic electricity and water, no work, no reconstruction, poorly funded schools, hospitals without medicines. As we meet there is no electricity or water in his neighborhood. His younger brother has to bring water from a neighbor's house for us to wash with and to make *chai*. The *diwan* is cold and dark. The sheikh apologizes for the dry tap and cold, dim room, illuminated only through a vine-covered front window. "The money of my country is still in only a few hands. And is still used only to pay spies and servants," explains the sheikh.

"The Americans are freak people. They try to insult us. They don't know anything about our way of life or how to treat people. They do not know how to treat Iraqis," says the sheikh in a tone of genuine concern. The sheikh is calm, articulate, focused; he is a man with an intense personal charisma. "They cover their faces with black masks and walk into homes and mosques in their boots. They urinate on mosques. They uncover and touch and insult Iraqi women. For our people, for a good Muslim man, he would rather die than allow a US soldier into his bedroom with his wife half-naked."

US troops had searched the sheikh's home over the summer, and along with rifling through his books and personal quarters they had seized his computer. Echoing a turn of phrase I'd heard elsewhere he adds, "The American soldiers are acting like monsters." The sheikh says that when Americans search a home they immediately go for the books, and he gestures to his own books. "They threw them all on the floor, even the holy Koran. They seem to know nothing about us—they can't even tell the Koran from other books."

The aesthetics of Islam (particularly Sunni Islam) do not typically represent God and the cast of spiritual notables in the visual way most Christian faiths do, with the cross, images of Jesus, Mary, the saints, and stories from the Bible. Instead, the Koran, the word of God as told to the Prophet Muhammad, becomes a representation of God: thus the attention to, and decoration of, words and verses within the culture of Islam. In an abstract way, the Koran even embodies God. This reverence for words both spoken and written has its deepest roots in the poetic traditions of the Bedouins. Though Christians revere the Bible, Islam imbues the physical form and object qualities of the Koran with a different, more intense political, spiritual and aesthetic significance that is not fully captured by the simple equation Koran = Bible.

It is this complex relationship to the book and its scholarly traditions that now animates the sheikh: "They kick the holy Koran, and rip its pages and throw it to the ground. That means they do not respect Islam. They do not respect us. They do not respect our culture."

The abstract pieces of an argument about culture, dignity, knowledge and politics are suddenly and horribly concrete. I imagine some foreign force, or just the NYPD, ransacking my bookshelves back in New York, smashing the few pieces of art I own and strip-searching my girlfriend.

At one point, when *chai* is served, Akeel moves a small table and in the process pulls off its top. "You're so strong. You should be with the resistance," says the sheikh slyly. Akeel giggles and does not translate the comment until a few moments later when the sheikh is talking to another cousin who has just arrived. Then from behind the wall the unseen women of the sheikh's family release a sweetly confident little boy of four with big brown eyes—the sheikh's son.

As a religious man in Ramadi, Dr. Letief is suspected of involvement with the resistance. A man of his position would not likely plant IEDs, but there is no doubt that there are men at his mosque who are fighters. The Americans know this—that's why they seized Dr. Letief's computer and keep a close eye on his mosque.

"The troops treat us like we were the right hand of Saddam," says the sheikh. "But we suffered under Saddam. We do not struggle for Saddam, but for our country and because we love our country. We suffered in the past and we suffer now." He tells the story of a young boy who threw a rock at a tank. In response the soldiers fired on a nearby mosque, his mosque, and demanded that the people there hand over the child.

"The soldiers said, 'You are all responsible, all the adults are responsible for the boy's actions.'" It is that new American drug-war, zero-tolerance fashion of thinking. I imagine the soldier hearing the Clintonesque voice of his superego: *It takes a village to get a child to throw a stone at my tank.*

The sheikh offers another story: "They know nothing. For example, we have many mosques here: the Mosque of The Eight, the Abu Had Mosque and al-Jihad Mosque. The Americans arrested the sheikh of al-Jihad Mosque simply because of its name, Jihad. They think that means 'war.' It means 'struggle in the path of God.'"

The detained sheikh was named Wasmi Khasim Hussein. He was sixty-eight when the GIs hauled him off to the local jail with some of his students. There he was beaten and humiliated in front of the pupils. Between his high blood pressure, the beatings and the sleep deprivation Sheikh Wasmi Khasim Hussein ended up dead.

Then Dr. Letief's cousin, a quiet young man in a long leather jacket, produces Wasmi Khasim Hussein's file and gives me a copy of his detention photo: a bald-headed man, eyes cast upward, hands behind his back, stands against a wall. Below the photocopied picture of Hussein is his full name in English, a "patient number," and a note reading "see SSG [staff sergeant] Comingo" followed by a military-only phone number. The next photocopy snapshot shows a photo of Khasim Hussein dead, naked, his face swollen. On his chest is a sign identifying Khasim Hussein as an enemy prisoner of war: "EPW 458, July 18 '03."

"This is one of the cases we are working hard on. We are trying to get justice; we want compensation for the family, and we want the soldier who killed him to be punished," says the sheikh. So far progress has been very slow.

Perhaps Khasim Hussein was with the resistance, or perhaps he wasn't. But his death in custody and his humiliation in front of his pupils no doubt served to recruit many young men to *al-mujahadeen*. When the dead sheikh's students were released from detention and came home to a town with no services, no reconstruction, limited power and water supplies, and empty clinics, some of them no doubt "put their names on the list," as Iraqis say, and awaited orders from the armed underground.

Sheikh Letief wants us to meet a family that was, he says, unjustly raided and had many members killed. As we drive east toward Habbaniya beneath the still dusty brown sky with palm trees and reeds bending in the wind, we pass the edge of a large cordon search operation. Elements of the 82nd Airborne's Task Force All American (then operating around Ramadi) are at work. Several Humvees with mounted guns hold the perimeter while a squad of soldiers leads a boy of about ten toward a Bradley. We skirt around the scene and roll down a rutted dirt side road under a canopy of widely spaced date palms into the village of al-Sigaria. Nearby is an old British airbase and a place called Camp Coolie.

In July US troops raided the family compound of a farmer named Shaaker Mahmoud Moklef and, in what seemed like a moment of panic and overreaction, shot down almost the entire family. When Shaaker's home was raided he, his wife Tahal Thumal and their adult son ran into the courtyard thinking they were being robbed. From the other side came young GIs with guns blazing. The unarmed family was cut down. We are shown the compound where they fell. Some dried drops of blood still splatter the wall. The surviving family members seem to be keeping these as evidence. The courtyard's old metal door has been blown open with an explosive charge.

Shaaker was suspected of making IEDs. The sheikh says no weapons or bomb-making supplies were found at the compound. In the shooting Shaaker's daughter Ala was hit in the arm. The killings seem to have been a mistake, and the troops involved tried to cover their tracks. Ala, her arm bandaged, was put on a chopper with the corpses of her mother, father and brother and flown to the military hospital in Babel. She was treated and sent home, while the corpses were introduced into the labyrinthine archipelago of US army morgues, hospitals, collective graves and hostile bureaucracies.

Ala is now the responsibility of her uncle's family, one of Shaaker's brothers, Ali Moklef. Uncle Ali wears a dark winter robe and the red-checked headscarf. His face is puffy, and he has a graying mustache, no beard.

It was Ali who shouldered the task of finding and retrieving the bodies of his brother's family. This proved to be a vexing job involving endless waiting, the military runaround, long stints of travel, lots of filling out of forms and struggling with bad translation. Sheikh Letief helped Ali in all of this using what influence he had among those involved. Eventually Shaaker's body was recovered from the morgue of the civilian hospital to which it had been transferred without explanation. The corpse of Tahal, Shaaker's wife, was finally exhumed from a collective grave at the military hospital in Babel some weeks later.

"They bound her hands when they buried her," says Ali. "She was not in a coffin, only wrapped in plastic. The soldiers would not bring her body home in an ambulance. They just brought her to the checkpoint. I had to find a taxicab that would bring her body back. It is a long drive, an hour and a half."

I try to imagine the horror of forcing the stiff, decomposing, dirt-covered corpse of one's sister-in-law into the back seat or trunk of a taxicab. How does one get a corpse into a taxicab? How does one ask a cabbie to help transport the rotting human remains of a relative? The body of Ali's nephew is still missing.

"We don't know where the boy is."

Standing in the courtyard with various male relatives milling around, Rob and I take notes and shoot some video. Soon our questions fall flat. The faces of our hosts are slack and emotionally empty. Ali points to Ala, who is standing politely in a black *abaya* and *hejab,* her hands folded in front of her. "Ala was very smart, the best in her class. Now she is last. She only gets zeros. She cannot concentrate." Ala begins to cry.

There are offices in Baghdad for "rectifying" problems like these. They are called the Civil Military Operations Centers, or CMOCs. But as Rob found out when he did a story on the CMOCs, the "offices" are often just some folding tables in a parking lot staffed by overwhelmed and hostile GIs from the 1st Armored Division. Furthermore, these CMOC offices are open for only a few hours a day a few days a week, and all of them are in Baghdad.

Uncle Ali has been to a CMOC; they lost his paperwork. Ali and Sheikh Letief have been pressuring as best they can for some sort of redress, compensation and acknowledgment of wrongdoing. They pursue American and Iraqi channels, methods both formal and informal. Ali found his sister-in-law's body by beseeching Iraqi doctors and morgue staff to look at his family photos. A mortician had recognized Tahal, the murdered mother of the family, and with no help from the military had her corpse exhumed. In the therapy culture of America we would say that Ali and the sheikh are looking for some closure.

Horribly, Ali's situation is not unique in the New Iraq. An English-language human rights report issued jointly by the National Association for the Defense of Human Rights in Iraq and the now-defunct Occupation Watch offers the following summary of another mistaken shooting and harrowing corpse recovery.

Mazen Antoine Hanna Noraddin was a thirty-two-year-old Christian sales representative for a pharmaceutical company and at times a translator for the US army. He lived with his wife and two daughters. Mazen was headed to work with his pharmaceutical sample case in hand when he was cut down in the crossfire of a shootout during a resistance ambush of an American patrol. Mazen, it seems, was killed by the American return fire. Below is the relevant part of the Occupation Watch/DHRI report:

> The unit [responsible for the shooting] must bring the corpse to [the military base at] the airport for forensic examination. They allow Mazen's father to accompany the body. Fortunately, he speaks and understands some English. He waits two hours at the airport before being told he can take his son's corpse home—by taxi. Mr. Antoine—Mazen's father, 72 years old—refuses, telling the soldiers that no taxi driver will pick him up with a corpse and that it is hard to find taxis near the airport to begin with. After some discussion, the same unit received the order to return Mazen's body and his father to his home, but they insist he get out at the nearest intersection instead. Mazen's father, told to carry the body the rest of the way, replied that he cannot and that there is no problem in reaching the house. His impression is that the soldiers are afraid. He insists and the unit agrees on the condition he runs in front of the truck—a human shield.
>
> When the unit reaches Mazen's road, they stop again, and this time they refuse to go ahead, and some friends on the street assist Mazen's father in carrying the body back to the house.

Despite much effort by Abu Mazen, compensation for this case was re-
jected by a CMOC on November 21, 2003.

A s we leave the Moklef compound, our interviews complete, Sheikh
Letief tells Akeel: "You will eat with me. I will take one of the
journalists as a hostage to make sure you come back to my house." The
sheikh's mouth curls in ever so slight a smile and he points to me. Akeel
laughs nervously and instead offers Rob, who is younger and whom Akeel
has not known as long. It is all very Iraqi.

"Rob, I think maybe you will go with the sheikh," says Akeel. Eshelman looks at the sheikh, then at Akeel, then at me. His eyes betray a
faint flicker of concern.

"We'll be right behind you. The sheikh just wants some company," I
tell him, not that I really know what's going on.

As we roll out Akeel explains how the sheikh used the word *hostage*. I
realize that it's just droll Iraqi humor, but it's still a bit unsettling. "I am
ashamed to say it, but I am glad you gave him Rob."

"Yeah, C.P.—he really wanted you. But I thought you wouldn't like
that."

When we arrive back in Sheikh Letief's dark *diwan* the smells of rich
food waft in from the back rooms where the women are cooking. I feel
bad for having doubted Dr. Letief even for a moment and feel ashamed
that perhaps he worried that we would not take his invitation seriously.
Before we eat, the sheikh performs his afternoon prayers at one side of
the dark room facing south toward Mecca. Then his young cousin in the
black leather coat comes in and unrolls a floral printed oilcloth across
the floor. Next come the heaped communal plates of roast chicken, rice,
beans, pickles, salad, bowls of soup, hot peppers and warm flatbread.

All this is served by the sheikh's young cousin; the women stay hidden. We move cushions from the wooden couches to the floor and, after a moment of waiting for all the dishes to arrive and for the sheikh to start, we dig in. The women will eat what we do not finish—the bad side of Bedouin culture.

When the extra food and empty plates have been returned and the rounds of strong, sweet tea are brought out on a tin tray, and the light begins to fade, we stand and prepare to leave, beginning the rounds of long good-byes and solemn pledges to return. As we talk and rustle around a wail begins to rise from the back rooms. The sheikh's four-year-old son is weeping, screaming inconsolably on the other side of the thin wall. Finally the unseen women let the boy into the *diwan*. He rushes to his father, his little face contorted and streaked with tears.

"What's wrong with the little guy?"

"He thinks you and Rob are here to take his father. He is saying, 'Don't go, the Americans will kill you,'" explains Akeel, lighting a cigarette nervously. The sheikh gathers the boy in his arms and tries to calm him: *"La, la, habibi.* They are our friends. It's OK."

Searching, breaking, humiliating, intimidating and killing are, after all, the quotidian details of military occupation. In Iraq the examples seem endless, so here's one more story.

In Baghdad's Kadamiya neighborhood, a working-class Shia district, Rob and I meet another family suffering from an encounter with trigger-happy GIs. Abu Sammar Razak Juwad keeps his son's bullet-ridden white sedan in the gated driveway of his solid cement home. Abu Sammar's son Abdel Wahab was killed by US troops while approaching a checkpoint. Abu Sammar is short and thin with a deeply lined face; he wears a loose white turban. The story of his son's demise is typical: it involves brutality, death and bereavement, but also the bureaucratic humiliation of the survivors. Over the customary glasses of strong, sweet *chai,* the victim's older brother Sammar Abdel Razak Juwad recounts the tale of Abdel Wahab's disappearance.

On July 13, 2003, Abdel, a freelance machinist and repairman, never came home from work. Days later his family found his bullet-riddled and blood-soaked car parked by the side of a road along a canal. They had no idea what had happened. Was Abdel dead or wounded and in some hospital? Had he even been driving the car? Who shot up the car: Thieves? Police? Soldiers? The mystery went unsolved despite the family's inquiries with hospitals, police, courts, the military and other agencies. For almost two months they had no idea what had happened; they feared the worst, and hoped for the best.

Then Abdel's brother, Sammar, overheard a man on a bus discussing a shooting he'd witnessed at a checkpoint near the place where Abdel's car was found. The man, Mazzan Jomal Atia, had been an interpreter for the US military during the summer of 2003. He was distressed and haunted by some of what he had seen and had quit as a result. Now he was randomly unburdening himself to a stranger on the bus when Sammar overheard. By chance Sammar had stumbled upon a witness to his brother's murder.

Mazzan Jomal Atia, the former interpreter, lives with his family in a cinder-block house on the outskirts of Sadr City, not far from an American base called Camp War Eagle. I went down the neighborhood's rutted streets to find Atia but only made contact with his brother, who confirmed the story. Sammar gave me a copy of a sworn affidavit in which Mazzan Jomal Atia describes the murder of Abdel Wahab. It reads as follows:

About 6 am on July 13th 2003 I went on patrol no. 14 with Lieutenant Yorker which lasted until 8 pm that day, we were joined by another patrol under the same number led by Lieutenant Pistwin where they set up a road block in an unsuitable place and time as it was getting dark and it was the canal highway where drivers usually drive fast on that road. They set up obstacles to make the road narrow so they could control the oncoming traffic, as a result there was a long queue of cars and as a result of that the oncoming traffic was unable to see the checkpoint clearly.

After checking a few cars, darkness fell which made the situation worse for both drivers and the soldiers controlling the checkpoint. All of a sudden I saw a white car coming forward, but turned right just before reaching the checkpoint to avoid other cars which were already there… I thought this was the right thing to do, but the American soldiers fired at him. The driver lost control of the car and drove towards the checkpoint slowly until the car was very close to the checkpoint, the soldiers fired at the car when it was about 70 meters away from them.

Lieutenant Pistwin shouted to the driver to get out of the car but the driver made no move to get out of the car. I turned to the officer and said: how can he get out? He is dead. The officer came close to the car opened the car door and pulled the driver from it by his shirt and dragged him along the street without any respect as he was bleeding from the head and chest. He dragged [him] for more than twenty meters, and gave orders to two of his soldier to watch him and ordered the soldiers to search the car hoping to find any excuse that can justify the shooting they did not find anything not even a knife.

The soldiers spent about more than half an hour searching the car leaving the man bleeding heavily, while two soldiers of which one of them was a woman soldier stood by the man chatting and laughing, which really made me very upset. I asked them why they were laughing and pointing their weapons toward the man while he was in this state and asked them again: are you afraid of him?

So they stopped and turned their weapons away from him. I searched the man and found his ID card, he was Abdel Wahab Abin and I could not read his last name as the bullet had gone through the card and destroyed that part of it.

Capt. Head the leader of the patrol no 14 arrived on the scene also the leader of the camp who I only know as the Colonel. He ordered the soldiers to send the MPs away from the place at once without knowing any details about the shooting.

A reporter arrived at the scene by chance, he tried to take pictures, but was threatened not to do so and ordered to leave at once. The Colonel told me to take the reporter away from the scene and not to say anything to him against us, but I told the reporter that they have killed the man deliberately without mercy, he had no fault at all, he just tried to avoid colliding with the other cars and the checkpoint.

A soldier came and tried to take the man's shirt off to count the number of bullet holes which hit him, the man raised his hand as if to ask for help, but the soldier pushed his hand away violently and ripped his shirt off to count the bullets. Then he was put on a stretcher and a drip feed was attached to him. He was strapped on the car bonnet and was taken to the American military hospital, they asked me to come and have a drink of water or soft drink as I was in a bad state but I refused. I put his ID card in his car in the hope that his family might find it and asked the people on the scene to help me push his car off the road. I asked Lieutenant Yorker to write down my name, that of the MP and the wounded man's name. I didn't know why.

In the next day they asked me to go with them on Patrol as normal but I refused and told them that I was in a bad state because of what happened the night before. After they left I went to talk to the person responsible for the translators and told him that I did not wish to continue this job. The patrol returned to camp and they said they have cancelled the patrol duty that day because I refused to go with them, we met at the officer in charge office and I surrendered my Translator ID card to them.

When I was asked about the reason I replied, "Just to help the Iraqi people." The patrol officer took me aside and asked me if he had done something wrong to me and if I have any ill feeling towards him. I told him no. After that he said that [he] had heard them saying that the man who was shot was drunk. I said he was not as I was there and I saw what happened.

At this point the affidavit starts naming the soldiers involved. As I hold the Arabic version of the deposition in the *diwan* of Abu Sammar's home, the bereaved father explains the story: "The translator says they let my son bleed for forty-five minutes before the soldiers drove him to the hospital. Wahab died the next day at Baghdad's al-Jedida police station and they put him in the police morgue. They could have saved my son but they let him die."

From the al-Jedida police station Wahab's body was taken to Najaf and buried by some of the officers, who somehow knew or guessed that Wahab was Shia. It is Shia custom to honor the dead with burial in the holy city of Najaf, where Imam Ali was martyred. Bodies from all over Iraq are shipped to Najaf for interment, and the city is said to hold the world's largest cemetery.

As is always the case with real tragedies, the details of the story are full of weird, irrational twists—for example, the police aiding the US military in a cover-up but then honoring the body with burial in Najaf. The old man goes on to explain how at first he had liked the Americans and gave their patrols water. He had hated Saddam, but now everything has reversed.

"They are the terrorists. I want them punished by international law. They killed my son and they didn't even tell me."

How does one properly end such an interview? I never could get the technique right. Often these my-son-is-dead-thanks-to-your-freedom interviews do not properly "conclude" or "wrap up," they just dissolve into awkward silence, back where it all began. Abdel Wahab Razak Juwad was dead when we arrived, he is still dead, and he will be dead tomorrow. The old man's eyes are vacant with rage. He takes another deep drag on his cigarette and looks at me from the other end of the hard wooden couch.

10

Things Fall Apart

The people of England have been led in Mesopotamia into a trap from which it will be hard to escape with dignity and honour. They have been tricked into it by a steady withholding of information. The Baghdad communiqués are belated, insincere, incomplete. Things have been far worse than we have been told, our administration more bloody and inefficient than the public knows. It is a disgrace to our imperial record, and may soon be too inflamed for any ordinary cure. We are to-day not far from a disaster.

T. E. Lawrence, "A Report on Mesopotamia,"
The Sunday Times, August 22, 1920

A young white South African pilot leans in the cockpit doorway of a small NGO-chartered prop plane and gives his passengers the pre-flight pep talk: "At 10,000 feet above Baghdad International Airport, we will begin our descent in a spiral dive. This avoids surface-to-air missiles and ground fire, we hope. But don't worry—the maneuver is well within the technical capacities of the machine. Enjoy the flight to Baghdad."

The flight is fine—but the dive is fast, steep and scary.

It is early June 2004. Since April most roads into the capital of Iraq have been closed by sporadic combat and marauding gangs of looters.

Westerners are special targets. Some elements in the resistance are said to pay $20,000 a head for hostages. The only truly open road is the heavily patrolled route north through Kurdistan to Turkey or Iran.

I am headed back for my third trip to Iraq, and like most journalists now, I am flying in. It's the "safe" way to reach Baghdad, a politically diseased metropolis that, after fourteen months of US occupation and alleged reconstruction, is still tormented by a fever of violence, social breakdown, administrative anarchy and economic decline. The crisis now seems to feed on itself in an epidemic fashion, with symptoms reinforcing root causes in a downward spiral. Lack of security—the central issue—means lack of electricity, which means no work, which means more violence, and so the spiral continues. In response, Iraqis either cling to a blind faith that America will sort things out, or turn increasingly to tradition, self-organization, Islam and armed resistance.

At the 1970s-style passenger terminal where we land, the long hallways and lounges are empty. Outside I find some Kroll security men headed to Baghdad and bum a ride. The twenty-kilometer dash from here to the city is called "RPG alley." This, despite the airport being contained within a huge US military base.

"This road is ridiculous," says the flak-jacketed Brit riding shotgun. He chambers a round in his Heckler & Koch assault rifle. Recent ambushes have hit several convoys here. The only one that made the news ended with four more dead mercenaries from Blackwater Inc., their SUV in flames. "The 1st Cav should have checkpoints every few clicks. I have no idea how they think this is supposed to work without a secure airport."

It's been a bad month. The malady of occupation is in full recrudescence: car bombs killing scores each week, assassins culling the political class, routine but underreported sabotage. In the slums of east Baghdad—Sadr City—the newly arrived 1st Cavalry Division has almost nightly shootouts with Muqtada al-Sadr's Mahdi Army.

The only journalists from the Agadeer crew who have come back recently are Dahr Jamail and Dave Enders (Akeel has escaped to the UK and
married the social worker). The three of us are bivouacked in a cheap, almost empty Baghdad hotel run by a friendly but thuggish man from Falluja. The accommodations—along with our recently grown beards, dark
tans, locally purchased clothes and preference for beat-up old cars—are
all part of a low-tech "security strategy." If most Western journalists live
in walled compounds with armed guards and still get kidnapped or shot
up, we figure that our best bet is to do the opposite. Go local, blend in, try
to pass as Iraqi, to the extent that we are able.

It's just ten days to sovereignty and the city waits. I awake, as usual, in
a sweat to the sound of a rumbling boom. The big explosions usually
occur in the morning. This one sounds close. "Car bomb!" yells Dahr
from down the hall.

"Abu Talat called. The bomb was right by where his wife works. He's
headed over," says Dahr. "We're outta here in five minutes." At al-Rashid
Street, in old Baghdad, blocks from the Central Bank of Iraq, we find the
aftermath. It wasn't a car bomb, just a big IED set to hit a money truck.
But the timing was off by a few seconds, and commuters took the blast
instead. Four are wounded, and one may have already died.

Iraqi cops and bank security men with Kalashnikovs mill around a
smashed wall and some twisted metal gates, while two Arab TV crews
shoot video. Thirty feet away sits a victim's shattered car. Looters are already at work stripping the salvageable parts. The cops pay no attention.

Thanks in part to police inaction, kidnapping, carjacking and murder
impose an informal dusk-to-dawn curfew in many parts of this city. The

director of the Baghdad morgue tells me that he now sees an average of at least 600 unsolved murders every month, adding, "There are many more cases we don't receive." In a city of roughly 4 million, this translates into a crime rate about ten or fifteen times higher than the most violent cities in America—a crime rate that has serious economic consequences.

"Little things create big economic problems," explains Asaad Witwit, an elegant but casual Iraqi burgher who owns four factories, three of which are currently closed. "Security is the biggest problem." We're meeting in the riverfront offices of the Iraqi Federation of Industry, a lobby group for private-sector manufacturers.

Witwit is a leading board member. As we speak in English, three of his colleagues are working the phones in fast, angry Arabic. The federation just bought a new, truck-sized generator for its building, but the machine was stolen before it was even delivered. (US contractors deal with such problems by giving their mobile phone numbers to local sheikhs so they can have first dibs on buying back their gear.) Iraq's badly battered infrastructure is another problem, explains Witwit. "For example, you cannot make paint if you do not have clean water. Salts and minerals in the water ruin the paint. Or to make ice, or can food, or process meat, you need clean water. We don't have that," he says philosophically. Behind him his colleagues rage on in Arabic about the "son of a whore" who sold them the generator and then most likely stole it back himself.

Then there are the cheap imports that have flooded the country since the US invasion. Witwit's sole working factory is a plastics plant that makes thermoses and coolers, but he has laid off most of his thirty employees because Chinese and Iranian imports are driving down prices. Upgrading and retooling would require capital. "We need loan programs, investment, but the Americans do nothing. They only talk about the free market." In the meantime, the violence escalates.

The main road into Baquba, thirty miles northeast of Baghdad, is closed by US Army Humvees and tanks. A column of smoke rises from the outskirts of the city. It's mid-morning on Thursday, June 24— less than a week before the handover of sovereignty in Iraq—and the day is turning out to be hot, hazy and violent.

Four major Iraqi towns have broken out into open rebellion. In the north, Mosul is ripped by five car bombs, leaving more than 200 wounded and many dead. To the west, in Falluja, insurgents repel a Marine assault and withstand aerial bombing, while farther west, in Ramadi, the resistance attacks several police stations. Other small attacks are reported in hamlets throughout central Iraq.

In Baquba, where the rebellion is most intense, the action begins at 5 a.m., when local *mujahadeen* attack a US patrol with RPGs, killing two GIs and wounding seven. Forty-five minutes later, *mujahadeen* units overrun and destroy part of the police station, killing an estimated twenty Iraqis, seven of them cops. The US military responds by dropping three 500-pound bombs on *muj* positions near the Baquba soccer field. By midday, US Army spokesman Brig. Gen. Mark Kimmitt is admitting that Baquba is out of US control.

By 10 a.m. Dahr, Abu Talat and I are headed north from Baghdad to Baquba. All we've heard are rumors that there's unrest to the south of Baquba, with civilian casualties arriving at the local hospital. We'll try to enter the city and visit the hospital to see what's going on. At the town's main entrance we bypass the first US military roadblock to try approaching from further east. Five miles on, there's another roadblock. A small cluster of cars and trucks idle in a fearful knot. Across some 500 yards of empty, shimmering blacktop sit two mean-looking Humvees, their guns pointed at the stalled traffic.

"The city is closed," says an Iraqi trucker, throwing his hands up in frustration. But after a moment we see dust rising from a rough plain of cropland and irrigation canals to the south. A few vehicles are leaving Baquba, and a few others are headed in the opposite direction, trying to circumvent the blockade by crossing the fields on rutted farming roads.

We follow the dust, heading off the main road through the fields and then through the street grid of a flattened and overgrown former Iraqi military base. The facility was destroyed during the US invasion of 2003; now poor squatters live in the few barracks still standing.

In the sky to our left, beyond some palm groves, appear two Apache helicopter gunships circling low over Baquba, occasionally dipping and diving; they look like they are strafing. The situation seems worse than we had thought, but we drive on.

Then, several hundred yards ahead, we see a Bradley Fighting Vehicle parked in an empty lot, facing out, toward us. From behind it, along a tree-lined street, come five tanks. Just as we turn right, away from the Bradley, three or four shots crack past our car in what feels like a long, slow succession. In the back seat, I hit the floor. Luckily, the right turn puts some buildings between us and the Bradley that fired at us, or perhaps over us.

"That was not the sound of the gun. That was bullets passing us," says Abu Talat, a tough but jolly retired army captain. That means the rounds were close. The tanks seem to be following us, but then they continue past as we turn again along a street with trees, some walls and the first real houses on the edge of Baquba. At this point we don't dare turn back or continue along the edge of the town.

"Fuck! What have we gotten into?"

As the numb fear from the close call with the Bradley fades, I begin to feel trapped and sick with dread. Even Abu Talat seems nervous. Dahr, on the other hand, seems to have simply switched off the fear; he smokes cigarettes and scans the scene in silence. Overhead we hear drones, and from our left the occasional clatter of the Apache choppers, but there is no gunfire in the streets, no armed fighters in sight. It is eerily calm. In the heart of the city the streets are empty and all the shops are shuttered. The few cars we see are usually taxis full of young men cruising around—probably *mujahadeen* patrols. Some of them eye us suspiciously.

"Boys, we are in a bad situation. Yes, very bad," says Abu Talat, as if commenting on the intense heat. The goal now is to find a certain religious sheikh we know before running into any *mujahadeen* checkpoints. The local fighters might be cool—or they might kill us.

The sheikh's store is closed, but we interview two men standing in front of it. They tell us about the dawn attacks and claim that the *muj* hold the city and that US forces have been driven out. We keep looking for the sheikh, asking questions of the few men we see on the streets. They tell us that the chief of police has had his home burned down by *mujahadeen*.

We visit one mosque, then another. At the second mosque, an old man, Haji Feissal, agrees to take us to the sheikh's home by a circuitous drive through the empty market. He says that there have been sporadic firefights and some tank incursions all morning.

We head deeper still into Baquba's narrow side streets, closer to the Apaches. As we cross each intersection, our nerves are taut with anxiety: we don't know who or what is down the next street. But we have to find the sheikh, since that's how things are done in Iraq. If you know an important local your chances of survival go up dramatically. If you wander around alone without contacts, you find trouble.

By the grace of God our friend the sheikh is at home and receives us warmly; he even speaks English. He demands that we stay for lunch and tea in his *diwan*. The walls are painted blue and decorated with a beautiful Chinese print, a framed Koranic verse, and a small piece of thrift-store-style art, a big-eyed portrait of a coy little girl.

In the past four days US forces had been conducting operations just south of town. Apart from fighting in the Baghdad neighborhood of Sadr City and some IEDs in al-Anbar, it was the only real combat occurring in the past week. We ask if this fighting is related to the US operations.

"No, this time the *mujahadeen* attacked. The United States is on the defensive," says the sheikh. "The resistance sent out fliers warning us to stay in today, and they attacked at dawn." At several points our interview is interrupted by a series of huge, extremely loud explosions that sound very close.

"Mr. Christian, do not be so scared," says the sheikh. "These are just for sound, to scare us. But for us, we've had so much war it is normal." He's so calm I start suspecting that he's high on Valium.

The sheikh says that the Americans cut power to the whole city as part of their siege, but other than that his story is similar to the one offered by the 1st Infantry Division: the *muj* attacked first and the United States responded with tanks, helicopters and warplanes, but US forces are still stuck on the edge of town.

"The fighters here are very well armed and well prepared. They have Kalashnikovs and RPGs," says the sheikh. Why this uprising? "We do not like the occupation. Look, everything is smashed—no electricity, no security, nothing gets fixed. People have no work. They are sick of waiting. The Tartars occupied us, the Turks occupied us, the British. All were driven out. The West cannot win this fight."

The sheikh's brother adds: "When the resistance is from inside Iraq I put my hand with them. But we do not like the foreign fighters, the Saudis or Syrians." He is simultaneously dismissing claims that al-Qaeda is running the Iraqi rebellion and acknowledging the controversial presence of internationalist *mujahadeen* in the country.

Lunch is served. We sit on cushions on the floor and eat from a big tray. Then tea is served, and we get a disquisition from the sheikh on all the secular aspects of the Koran. Outside, things have quieted down. It's been an hour at least with no bombs, no shooting, and no choppers overhead. The sheikh's brother reports that fifteen or more civilians are dead. We had wanted to go to the hospital, but it was too close to the *muj* positions downtown. We decide it's time to go before the fighting starts again. We thank the sheikh and start to leave.

"Every man has his fate," says the sheikh as we climb back into the car. "If you die here today it is the will of God. Don't worry. It is all in God's hands." For some reason, I do not find this comment reassuring.

The eucalyptus-lined main road out of Baquba is empty. Just before we get to the highway, we pass a car straddling the median. It's shot full of holes. A corpse is sprawled in the street, and the ground is covered in blood and oil. A hundred feet ahead are the obvious scars of tank or Bradley treadmarks and a heap of spent brass shells from a 50-caliber machine gun. We stop to take photos, but then Abu Talat sees a van and some men lurking in the trees near the road. "No, let's go," he says.

We drive away fast, then lurch to a halt. "Humvees!" says Abu Talat. I can't see them at first. They're about a quarter mile away, at the end of the wide, empty road. We pull over, not sure what to do. We have the *muj* behind us and trigger-happy US troops ahead.

We'll have to walk out. Dahr and I leave our gear with Abu Talat and—with our hands in the air, press passes held high—start a seemingly endless trek toward the US lines. The road is quiet, hot and bright. When we're equidistant between the fresh corpse behind us and the guns ahead, we start yelling, "American journalists—don't shoot!"

After what seems like a very long time we reach the line of GIs. They're mellow, spaced out from the heat, tired. Some of them seem a bit freaked out about having killed the motorist down the road. "He rammed a tank, that's why we lit him up," says one soldier. It seems an unlikely story— the car showed no sign of a collision. Perhaps the car was speeding and a soldier got scared, thought it was a car bomb, and opened up. The troops clear us to pass. I walk back for Abu Talat; they search the car, and then we race at top speed back to Baghdad.

"Boys, that was one hundred percent dangerous," chides Abu Talat, in his avuncular, military way. "But I think my wife will be very happy to see me when I get back tonight." He grins. And then, as if to warn us for real, he says, "You know, all the modern Iraqi revolutions—they always happen in July."

A day or two before Dahr and I go to Baquba a young guy named Tarek shows up at our hotel. He knew Dahr's editors and had met Rob Eshelman in Palestine. Tarek is an upper-middle-class Canadian medical student of Palestinian origin. He's a Muslim, fluent in Arabic and English, very smart, very young, very brave, and a bit naïve. He is an obsessive computer geek with a tendency toward pedantry on matters technological. Over the past two years he has spent several months in Palestine doing solidarity work.

The same day we get shot at in Baquba, Tarek—against the advice of even a pro-resistance ex-army officer—heads off to Falluja, a city controlled by the *mujahadeen* and under low-level US siege. In early May the US Marines had essentially given control of the city to the insurgents. But on June 24 fighting flared up again when US planes bombed several houses and the Marines tried to enter the city. That's the day that Tarek heads to Falluja.

His plan is to work in a civilian hospital. Once in Falluja, Tarek periodically calls in over the next few days to Dave and a filmmaker named Rick Rowley, who has also moved into our dive hotel. It seems Tarek has been intercepted by the local *muj;* they want to check him out before they let him work at the hospital. But with each call it seems they're still checking him out. (A few days into all this, Dahr leaves to return to Alaska. He's at the end of a three-month stint, and he is burned out and ready for some rest. He flies out on an NGO prop plane to Amman. All goes well on his flight, but the plane that departs just after his gets shot up with small-arms fire that kills one passenger and wounds several others.)

Tarek has been in Falluja for a week and it's been almost forty-eight hours since his last phone call. We are ready to hit the panic button when he finally shows up at the hotel. Tarek looks gaunt, smells bad, wears somebody else's clothes, and is totally freaked out. His description of Falluja, tinged with Stockholm-syndrome rationalizations, paints a picture of what can only be described as collective insanity. This is his story:

Tarek took a bus to Falluja, but before he could find the hospital he was intercepted by *mujahadeen* fighters and taken to the US-trained Iraqi Civil Defense Corps, made up of Iraqi army veterans, many of them former Baathists. The ICDC—renamed the Iraqi National Guard after the June 28 handover—asked him some questions, then deposited him with two "plainclothes" guys who turned out to be leaders of a *mujahadeen* cell. In Falluja, everyone is *mujahadeen:* the ICDC, the US-trained Iraqi police, and most of the people. More than anywhere else in Iraq, Falluja is tribal, religious and insular: a unique piece of the bigger picture.

The two men took charge of Tarek, telling him they had to check him out before he could do any medical work. For the rest of his stay in Falluja he was in the custody of a resistance cell made up of about ten local Falluja boys who had military experience but very little education. They had started their organizing and training a year before the US invasion.

Tarek repeatedly requested placement in a hospital or clinic but was instead held by this cell and given a tour of life among the fighters. Every few hours he was moved from house to house in cars packed with machine guns, rocket-propelled grenades, and what seemed to be heavily modified Sidewinder missiles (originally developed in the United States as air-to-air missiles, they had been taken from Iraqi warplanes by the *mujahadeen,* who now use them as mobile rockets).

"They were really nice guys," says Tarek. At first the nice guys were convinced that Tarek was a spy. The group tried to check his encrypted, Linux-loaded laptop but couldn't get it working. To save face, the local *muj* computer expert pretended that the laptop was OK, but then snagged it for safekeeping.

On the first day that Tarek was held—but "not as a hostage," as the *muj* cell kept telling him—they ran into a fighter who had been grazed by a bullet. Tarek was able to patch him up with no problem. The cell began to trust the med student—plus they were very impressed that he had a stethoscope.

"They really are simple people. Really," says Tarek, unwinding his tale in our hotel. "It's all about trust and family. They have no idea about security, technology. It is just God, kin and the nation. It's Alabama in Arabic. It really is."

Even though Tarek gained the trust of the cell, they lied to him and manipulated him every day, taking his passport and his computer, never delivering him to the hospital as they had promised and often taking him to the frontlines against his will. In Falluja the front is the north edge of town, along the Askari ("officers") neighborhood, which ends at the edge of Iraq's main east–west highway. In the desert on the other side of the highway were the US Marines in their armored vehicles. Most of the time the front was quiet, but at night it got busy. Tarek says that between five and seven *muj* fighters were being killed each day, usually by aerial bombing. During the first two days he was there the Marines attempted ground assaults, but thereafter mostly hung back (though ground combat continues). The *muj* would counterattack, but did not venture too far into the open desert. Tarek says that the whole time he was there, Falluja was buzzed by F-16 fighter jets and Predator drones. "The sound makes you crazy."

At night the cell would often head to the front to shoot at the Marines while dodging incoming US rounds. On most of these occasions they left Tarek behind, because he insisted that he only wanted to do civilian work. After each night of fighting the cell would turn on a little mechanical stuffed monkey that played a jingle. This was one of the few things Tarek was allowed to videotape on his small digital camera.

The culture of the local fighters, as described by Tarek, is a closed, selfreferential world. "They don't even watch the news," he tells us. "They just watch DVDs of sermons and speeches and *muj* music videos. Even the top guys had no idea what was going on in the rest of Iraq."

Of course, Tarek wasn't really sure who the top guys were. But there were hints. At one point in the fighting during Tarek's visit the ICDC actually told the *muj* irregulars to move to the wings and give them their heavy weapons. These US-trained professionals then did the bulk of the fighting against their would-be masters, the Marines. Tarek also says that the airstrikes on alleged safehouses in Falluja, such as the one on June 22 that killed about twenty people or the one on July 1 that killed four and wounded ten, were in fact precision strikes, in which spies had first dropped infrared beacons just before the attacks. Tarek says the victims were mostly foreign fighters, though not connected to the Jordanian terrorist Abu Musab al-Zarqawi, as the US military has claimed.

"People joked about Zarqawi," says Tarek. "There were foreign fighters in Falluja, and some were killed in those strikes. But I don't think Zarqawi was around. Falluja is very Iraqi."

Quite disturbingly, Tarek says that Sharia law—or perhaps more accurately, a kind of Sharia lawlessness—was in full effect in Falluja, with hands cut off for theft, women kept away from men, etc. Even worse was the routine killing of spies and suspected spies. The leader of the cell that watched over Tarek confessed one such crime to him.

Tarek, at the edge of a couch in our hotel, reads his notes quoting the man verbatim: "We are all sinners, Tarek, all of us, I swear. The things we've done make us sinners. There was a Turkoman who ran a hotel; he had a wife and family. We thought he was a spy, so we beat him. We broke every bone in his body, but he wouldn't confess. Then we cut a checkerboard in his back with a knife and poured salt on his wounds. He begged us to kill him but he would not confess. We knew by then that he was innocent. To kill him was an act of mercy. We are sinners all, Tarek."

Despite the Islamic motifs of life in Falluja, the *muj* there are not Taliban purists. The commanders all drive nice cars, BMWs and Mercedes. "No one has clean clothes, but the top guys are immaculate. They're just gangsters," says Tarek, switching momentarily from a tone of respect to one of disgust.

What comes through most clearly in his tale is the desperation of being under siege. "At one point they brought in this young guy who was dead. That night his mother, who just went nuts with grief, came out and woke her three other sons and told them to go the front, saying, 'Your brother is not dead. Finish his work.'"

When Tarek tried to talk politics with the *muj* he found them surprisingly uninformed and self-contradictory. At times they would say that Falluja would be the capital of a new Islamic state and that America would be destroyed. At other times they would admit that the only real solution to Iraq's occupation was political and that their military effort had limited effect.

Eventually a lower-ranking *muj* stole $400 from Tarek. There was an inquest, with lots of swearing on the Koran. It was clear who the culprit was, but once the Koran had been sworn on it was between the thief and God. Nonetheless, the man of the house in which the cell was then staying had his honor at stake (hospitality is hugely important in Iraq). The man, also a fighter, sold off some weapons and demanded that Tarek take the money. Tarek refused, which infuriated and demeaned his host. Finally Tarek agreed to accept part of the sum, which he then quietly left in the host's living room.

At this point Tarek negotiated the return of his passport and was finally allowed to work in a clinic (it was too dangerous to get to the main hospital). But by then the stress was getting to him. He told the cell commander that he needed to go back to Baghdad—to the hotel where I am staying, in fact—to think things over. The *muj* let him go but asked him to come back. Then they said they would bring his computer to the hotel (none of us was very happy about that idea).

"Tarek was kidnapped, but he is too proud to admit it," said the ex-military man who advised him against going to Falluja. "And he put your lives in danger, without asking or warning."

As Tarek recuperates in our hotel, he oscillates between flippant jokes and humble epiphanies about Iraq, war, himself, and the meaning of solidarity in a conflict where madness has become the norm.

11

Chaos the Sovereign

We are in for many more years of turmoil and misery in the Middle East, where one of the main problems is, to put it as plainly as possible, American power.

Edward Said, July 20, 2003

If Iraq's social geography were reduced to political antipodes, one pole would be the fortified and manicured Green Zone, the huge American-occupied palace and office complex originally built by Saddam. The other pole would be the fetid, baking east Baghdad slum of Sadr City, also known as al-Thawra (The Revolution).

A year into the occupation and entering the Green Zone is still like consuming a thousand-milligram tablet of denial washed down with fresh-squeezed orange juice. The air conditioning here is superb; everyone looks happy.

David Bourne is working on his laptop at the Iraqi Business Center, a near-empty, glass-walled subsection of the Convention Center. Bourne, wearing a crisp, medium-blue oxford shirt and dark slacks, exudes Ivy League confidence. His mission here is to do good and to do well at the same time.

"When we get the business center running, local subcontractors will be able to network and learn about bidding," he explains, as if the occupation weren't already fourteen months old. "A lot of the reconstruction hasn't begun yet, and the center will facilitate capacity-building with local firms." He pauses, and then adds with considered honesty: "A lot of Iraqis think it's just about who you know. But government-funded work requires competitive bidding, transparency, quality control, all that."

He won't comment on how Halliburton and Bechtel got their huge slices of the $18.5 billion reconstruction pie. But that's already a matter of public record. Bechtel got the first installment of its no-bid billion-dollar contract in April 2003, after secretive dealings with USAID.

On the other side of the glass wall, a uniformed janitor pushes a Zamboni-like buffer across a shining expanse of floor. Iraq seems a thousand miles away.

Now unplug from the Matrix: The temperature suddenly soars to a brutal 115 degrees Fahrenheit; the air reeks of sewage; and hot, furnace-like gusts blow grit into your eyes. An urbanized plain of misery and squalor opens before you, the hyperviolent Sadr City. The wide boulevards, laid down in the late 1950s by the optimistic planners of the Qasim regime, are now flooded for blocks at a stretch with ankle-deep pools of green, algae-rich sewage. Heaps of garbage smolder on the medians and in empty lots. Pirated electrical wires crisscross dense side streets of mud-brick homes. Small flocks of mangy goats and sheep, shepherded by women in flowing black *abayas,* forage in the trash.

The lumpen Shia who live here are derided by Baghdad's more urbane Sunnis as *sharugees*—an insulting term meaning "easterners" but connoting ignorance and filth. Like the N-word among some African Americans, *sharugee* has been defiantly appropriated by streetwise young Shiites for their own use.

The sewage problem in Sadr City is not merely unsightly: it is a major health threat. As the head of the local public works department, or Baladia, explains, the sewers here were never very effective, but the constant backup and nauseating overflow are new problems. First there was bomb damage; and then, as Baghdad's garbage trucks were looted or destroyed, trash clogged the sewers. Most of the trucks needed to clear the lines were also looted. The last four were recently commandeered by US contractors for use elsewhere. Bechtel has the $1.8 billion contract to rebuild Iraq's water, sewage and electrical systems. Electrical grid and water system work are also being done by Washington Group International. Local engineers say the firm has done next to nothing.

At Sadr City's al-Jawadir Hospital the halls are crowded with worried-looking men and women. An emaciated man with greenish skin is wheeled by on a gurney. Here one clearly sees the social impact of the sewer problem and the general chaos of which it is a subset.

The hospital director, Dr. Qasim al-Nuwesri, explains that the hospital serves at least a million and a half people and sees 3,000 patients a day, but lacks adequate medicine and medical equipment, clean water and security. "We have to get clean water shipped in," he says. "A German NGO delivers it in a tanker truck." Typhoid is rampant, he adds, and an outbreak of hepatitis E is gathering momentum, with forty new cases a week. "The coalition promises money and supplies, but there is never enough. I am forced to reuse needles and deny people anesthesia. We do only serious emergency surgeries."

Upstairs on one of the wards we meet a twenty-five-year-old internist named Ali Kadhem. Like many Iraqi doctors, he speaks English. His face is open and boyishly innocent, and he possesses an understated yet intense charisma. When he talks, the other doctors and orderlies watch and listen.

Ali says that gunmen frequently enter the hospital demanding special treatment for relatives. Two weeks ago an addict pulled a pistol on him and stole morphine. One doctor was shot by thieves right in front of the hospital. He says that since April, US troops have raided the wards on three different occasions, looking for wounded Mahdi Army fighters. "They interrogated the wounded and searched in a very rough way and tore down religious posters." Several wounded Mahdi men, as well as civilians, have fled the hospital in fear of the raids. "I know that some of these people died because they hid in their homes and we could not treat them," says Ali. "We could have saved them. The cause of all these problems is the Americans. We need for them to go."

The Mahdi uprising in Karbala and Najaf, provoked in large part by US assaults, alienated large sections of the mainstream Shiite community—particularly the merchant class, which depends on pilgrim traffic to the holy cities. But spend a day or two in al-Thawra and it's not hard to understand why people follow Muqtada al-Sadr. He is a junior religious scholar, unlike his father, who was an ayatollah, but Muqtada's leadership is primarily political, and his following is mainly Shiite but religiously diverse. His power is rooted in his willingness to oppose the occupation openly, just as his martyred father opposed Saddam.

More practically, he is followed because the branches of his organization deliver a small measure of order and stability to a few parts of Baghdad and cities farther south. In front of the hospital a man named Uda Mohame explains the logic: "Everyone cooperates with the Jeshi Mahdi. There are no police here, no government. The Mahdi direct traffic, they fix things, they do all the work."

At an office on one of al-Thawra's main streets I try to meet Muqtada's local representative, a twenty-nine-year-old sheikh named Hassan Edhary, but he is on the run. The 1st Cav wants him, dead or alive. His two predecessors are already in Abu Ghraib. A few weeks ago, US tanks blew up his office. Reconstruction started the next day at dawn.

"Little boys cleaned the bricks while the men rebuilt," explains a local man named Samir.

Now the walled compound, draped in black banners mourning the dead and topped with big fluttering green and black flags, looks as good as new. The men here are all Mahdi, but they are unarmed by day. There can be no formal interviews without the sheikh's permission. For the better part of a week I return again and again looking for Sheikh Edhary, but he's still on the lam. As I am leaving the office after one more failed attempt, a young Mahdi man says to me, "Look, the Americans attack us. That is why we fight. We have a right to respond."

It's late afternoon, and we're on another trip to Sadr City. Dahr and I and a translator named Samir roll out determined to find the Mahdi in action. They're out here somewhere—we've already seen a US patrol of two tanks and three armored Humvees.

On one of the slum's main thoroughfares, al-Radhewi Street, are several walls marked with a message in English. Big block letters read VIET-NAM STREET. Farther on, a wall bears a crudely painted mural depicting a modified version of an infamous Abu Ghraib torture photo. It is the prisoner in the hood and cloak standing on a box, arms outstretched, electrical wires dangling from his limbs. Next to him in the mural is the Statue of Liberty, but in place of her torch she holds the lever of an electrical switch connected to the wires. Below is scrawled "THE FREEDOM FORM GEORGE BOSH." We snap photos and move on.

Then, before we find them, the Mahdi Army find us. Two men in a sedan are suddenly next to us. "Pull over!" Now they are at our car doors, hands on the pistols in their waistbands. "Who are you? What are you doing here? Why are you photographing things?"

"Sahafee canadee, sahafee canadee!" I show them my counterfeit Canadian press pass. Our translator is talking fast, explaining that we are anti-occupation, that we are trying to show the truth. He's naming his family, naming sheikhs, naming Sadr men who are old friends. The undercover Mahdi guys fire back questions and suggest that we get out of the car. We show them the digital photos of the graffiti and offer to erase all the shots, but we ignore their request to get out. More fast Arabic. Finally the Mahdi begin to relax.

"This is called Vietnam Street because this is where we kill Americans," says one of them. "We are in a war with them. That is why we stopped you. You understand? We have to protect our people." The man in charge adjusts his pistol one more time, looks around, then says, "You can go." We thank them profusely and then hit the gas. The hard spike of adrenaline in my chest releases in a warm wash of endorphins.

The next day I head back looking for Sheikh Edhary, but he's still underground. On our way a pickup truck just ahead of us abruptly reverses into our taxicab with a slam, then does a three-point turn over the median. Suddenly everyone is backing up and turning around fast.

"Fighting ahead. We have to go!" says Hussein, a translator, journalist and computer hacker who hangs out with our ragtag crew. The next day Al-Jazeera reports that "around twenty Iraqi resistance fighters" were killed or wounded in clashes all over Sadr City.

There's more evidence of war at the offices of the District Advisory Council, a body elected in a hasty, poorly publicized, US-managed referendum. "Sorry, man. Nobody around. We're just here to secure the building," says Staff Sgt. Josh York. The twenty-five-member DAC dispersed several weeks ago after their leader was blown away in a political hit.

Now the council's compound is a small US firebase.

"They've been hitting us with RPGs every night," says Sergeant York. "No casualties yet, but last night we took eleven RPGs, one at a time all through the night." The young soldier doesn't look nervous or afraid, just beat-down tired.

Finally Sheik Edhary surfaces. Perhaps this has something to do with the Americans' new offer to allow al-Sadr's organization to participate in electoral politics. (The Sadr people are still quite cagey about what they will do on that front.) Edhary grants an interview, but mostly we just sit and watch him in action, Hussein quietly translating the conversations around us.

Edhary wears a white turban and flowing robes. His beard is full but short, like Muqtada al-Sadr's. He is dark, intense and very handsome. I can't help thinking that Edhary looks like a cinematically improved version of the real Muqtada al-Sadr, who is stooped, pudgy and frowning.

A stream of supplicants files through Edhary's little office, asking for advice, money and letters. One lives in a camp for internally displaced people and his shelter has no roof. Can the organization help? Edhary says, "I don't have enough people to go investigate your claim. But if you can find a religious sheikh in your area to write a letter on your behalf, then come back."

A young doctor explains that a group of medical workers has some money and wants to open a free or low-cost pharmacy to serve the people. Can the office contribute some money? The sheikh leans close and plays with his string of black prayer beads as the young man talks. Finally, he tells the doctor that Hussein, our hacker pal, can help the clinic with its computers. Hussein and the doctor exchange numbers.

Then come a few high-tension cell-phone calls. Some sweaty Mahdi fighters rush in. They've just busted looters with four stolen trucks full of sugar. It turns out that the trucks belong to a European NGO, not the government or some rich company. The sheikh wants the vehicles and sugar returned, via the police, to the NGO.

"We have the trucks in storage. Can we turn them over tomorrow?" asks the rotund Mahdi man in charge of the bust. He's wearing a dirty football jersey. "I am your servant. I have given my whole life to the religion, but I really cannot do this tonight."

Someone else bends over and whispers to the sheikh. Edhary looks worried. There's more whispering. Edhary leans away from the men at his desk and snaps taut a section of his black prayer beads, then counts the little glass balls. He is "asking God" for advice. An even bead count means yes; odd means no.

"No! No! Absolutely not," the sheikh bounces up from the desk, his black outer robe slipping from one shoulder. He's addressing the sweaty man. "The trucks must be returned tonight. If the trucks do not move now we will be blamed. Either you do it now, or just go and don't do it at all. I will find someone else." The sheikh is electric with stress but at the same time is dignified.

"I am your servant. As you wish," says the Mahdi guy, but he looks pissed as he and his posse sweep out to deal with the trucks.

If there is anything like "progress" in Iraq it takes place here, under the radar, in the rubble of occupation. Al-Sadr's followers, despite many faults, including thuggishness and misogyny, are central to creating what order there is in this ravaged ghetto.

On the last Friday before the handover I go back to Vietnam Street with Dave Enders for a mass prayer. This time, the Jeshi Mahdi are out in full force, armed with pistols and AK-47s. Line after line of them are politely and efficiently searching a crowd of more than 10,000 people who have come to lay their prayer mats in the street, worship and hear a political sermon. The Mahdi search us several times, and we are ushered to the front, walking barefoot across the solid field of prayer mats; some are mere towels, others are colorful, intricately patterned carpets. "I bet this is the first pair of Brooks Brothers socks that's ever touched down on Vietnam Street," quips Enders, pointing to his feet. The sermon, by an al-Sadr sheikh named Ous al-Khafji, attacks the occupation but asks the people to remain calm. The Mahdi have declared a cease-fire.

Under a blazing sun, with squads of men and boys spraying rose water on the congregants, the crowd chants, "Ya Allah, Ya Ali, Ya Hussein," meaning with Allah, etc., then "Muqtada! Muqtada! Muqtada!" At the end the worshipers all shake hands, then disperse.

Later I am granted an interview with some Mahdi fighters. They make sure I can't see where we are headed as we drive deep into the side streets of Sadr City. Our interview takes place in an abandoned shop; there are three fighters, two of whom were jailed and tortured under Saddam. They repeat the party line about wanting peace but add, "If the Americans arrest people, we will strike."

One of them moves a tarp and reveals a huge 155-millimeter artillery shell and a long spool of wire. It's an IED. "If they attack, we have this rat poison for the American rats," says the fighter, pointing to the bomb. "But, God willing, we will not be forced to use it." It's time for me to go.

Clearly sovereignty remains fragmented, localized, ephemeral—and mostly imaginary. Neither Iraqis nor the Americans have control. The new prime minister, Iyad Allawi, threatens to declare martial law. How he might impose martial law and how it would differ from the current methods of the occupation are difficult to envision. In the new Iraq, only chaos is truly sovereign.

12

Disneyland Burning

Fight for the sake of God those that fight against you, but do
not attack them first. God does not love the aggressors.

The Koran

The first thing I notice when Jayce Sellers pulls into the dirt parking
lot is the small Arabic-language Iraqi license plate on the front of
his truck. He has gained a little weight. Back in Baghdad, at the Club, he
looked gaunt. The three months home are showing.

"Yeah, it's the haji mo-baji," he says, pointing a thumb back to his truck
as we head toward a beachside bar. "I got the plate when we raided this
Fedaycen guy who had a whole command post set up in his house. He
had a bunch of Iraqi IDs and license plates." In the back seat of the "haji
mo-baji" Sellers has a new M-4 rifle with a mag light strapped to the barrel, Baghdad style. "It's all legal and shit, but you could easily make it fully
automatic. You never know when shit might jump off here."

Garrett and I are doing another short "embed," this time in north Florida. We are here for a number of reasons. One is to see the guys we met
in Iraq, but we also want to know what fighting in Iraq does to young
Americans, and by extension to America. Will these used and abused

vets return with the scales lifted from their eyes? Or will they clutch even tighter to the lies that sold the war, their macho sense of self and patriotic cachet all the more hardened?

After a day in Tallahassee with Tyler Brunelle, John Crawford and some of the other recently demobilized guys from the 3rd of the 124th, we've dropped down to Port St. Joe on the Panhandle's "Forgotten Coast" to find Sellers. The drive south from Tallahassee took us through the plantations of the mighty St. Joe Paper Company: mile after mile of scrawny, fast-growing pines planted in perfectly straight rows. Soon it will all be toilet paper—that is the specialty here. It's sobering: a vast industrial forest devoted solely to wiping asses.

Sellers is, as ever, the maverick, an artist at heart. We head to the bar's deck on the beach to order beer and raw oysters. "The visuals are usually pretty good here," he says, referring to the ladies. Sellers is warm and very candid about how he feels, about the difficulty of adjusting, about everything. He is working with the family sign-painting business and looking forward to going back to school next semester.

"My vocabulary just totally collapsed in Baghdad. I kinda feel dumb," he says. "You know, it's fucked up, but sometimes I miss Baghdad. Think about it. Over there you have the power to kill people, or more like, make 'em think you're gonna kill 'em. I get back here, I'm a civilian." During the first few weeks back, Sellers got into a few fistfights; one ended with him getting pepper-sprayed by a female cop.

Welcome home.

He relays the story common to all vets fresh from combat zones: fights, insomnia, occasional paranoia, heavy drinking, trouble with authority. But he's clearly getting it under control: he has weaned himself off Valium and is starting to sleep better, relate to his girlfriend and her kids, and get into his work. It is an impressive shift. And during our several hours by the beach none of us ends up too drunk.

But many vets can't cope. The Miles Foundation, which deals with domestic violence and sexual abuse in the military, reports that it gets 150 calls for assistance every week, compared to 75 calls a month before the wars in Afghanistan and Iraq started. The stories from Sellers, and from the guys up in Tallahassee and a few of the paratroopers from the 82nd Airborne who demobilized back to Fort Bragg, are at times both sad and chilling.

One guy tells of some heavy drinking that leads to a drive past his on-again-off-again-girlfriend's house. Out front is a strange pickup truck, some other man's vehicle. So the vet goes home, puts on his old desert battle uniform, sharpens up an Iraqi bayonet, and creeps through the night back to her house. "It was a good insertion," he says, using the military lingo. At the edge of her driveway the soldier "pops a squat" and starts some surveillance, slowly working himself into a lethal rage, getting ready for the attack.

Then he notices that the license plate of the truck is from the next state over, and he realizes to his shame and horror that it belongs to the woman's brother, who is visiting. A tragedy is averted.

Another guy tells the story of heading out for dinner with his lady when suddenly he is gripped by a combat-style premonition that his neighbors are about to break into his house. It's the feeling one gets about an undetected IED hidden in a heap of trash. He *knows* that something is wrong, out of place. In Iraq these flashes of intuition can save lives. The soldier grabs a pistol, drives to his father's and explains the situation, then the two of them head back to case the neighbor's house. But the neighbors aren't going anywhere and his house is fine. Nothing is wrong. It is just another quiet night in suburbia. Slowly the "premonition" dissolves.

In Tallahassee we hook up with Brunelle and Crawford. I had helped get a few of Crawford's stories published in a New York magazine, *The Brooklyn Rail*. Then I put him in touch with a literary agent, who has snagged him a huge book contract.

"Oh, that first part of the advance?" says Crawford with a mischievous grin. "Yeah, that's gone. The ex took part of it, and we've been partying pretty hard." A bunch of guys from Alpha Company have rented a ranch house together on a shaded side street. In the front room is a pool table, some couches, a TV and an American flag. The vets roll as a posse, watching each other's backs, helping each other mac on the young coeds and generally trying to unwind.

The afternoon starts at a frat-style drinking joint and turns into an evening and then a very late night as we relocate to several other venues, each one flowing with beer, packed with bleached blondes and vibrating with loud, nondescript rock and hip-hop. The beer arrives as big, plastic three-dollar pitchers of Bud Light. At one spot, refills are free if you wait in line.

On the way to our last stop with Tyler—who, ever the gentleman, is acting as our host—we are suddenly surrounded by hundreds of African American teenagers. They are yelling excitedly and running through the streets and across nearby lawns and parking lots. Behind them come some of Tallahassee's finest, with a "pop-pop-pop" firing paintball-style gas guns loaded with pepper-spray rounds. We park and wend our way through the mini-riot. It seems there had been a "phone party"—a spontaneous convergence by hundreds of high school students all in contact with each other by cell phone. The kids had filled a large McDonald's parking lot, and then someone called the police—too many black people in one place. As Tyler explains: "This is Florida, but it is still the South."

At the bar, a sprawling "Irish pub" full of kids from Tallahassee State, someone asks, "You guys come through all those coons on the way in?"

Bizarrely, this casual racism is the only spontaneous and organically political comment of the evening. This group of guys, recently forced to spend a year of their young lives fighting an imperial war with global implications, are politically mute. They are neither pro-war, hopped up on patriotism, nor bitter, cynical and anti-war. Even when prodded by my occasional questions they are reluctant, or unable, to discuss the larger politics of what they have just lived. "Yeah, I feel bad about it, but I don't really watch the news. At first I did, but I've stopped," says Gleason, a quiet, stocky guy who lives with Crawford. It is as if the very landscape of America has been flooded with an odorless, anesthetic gas that prohibits analysis. At one point, though, Crawford does say, "I get back and gas is $1.70 a gallon. What *were* we fighting for?" In conversation I realize that the only available script for most of these guys to process their experience with is the discourse of personal trauma. But they reject the trope of the damaged vet.

Hanging out on the quiet beach with Sellers I ask again what he thinks of the war. He looks away and then back. "To be honest, I am sort of confused. I am not sure what I think about it."

"But come on. You're not gonna vote for that draft dodger in the White House?" I ask, referring to George Bush.

"No, I guess not. But I don't know. I voted in a local referendum to give confined hogs more space," he says, as if offering a compromise. Then, without skipping a beat, he tells me to "scan right" as a young woman in a string bikini passes.

Camilo Mejia was also in the Florida National Guard, 1st Battalion of the 124th, which draws its troops from south Florida. His unit missed the invasion but was stationed out in Ramadi and saw some nasty action in the counterinsurgency. Camilo was a staff sergeant like Kreed Howell, in charge of eight guys.

In October 2003, after five months of kicking in doors, being in fire-fights, and helping to kill and imprison people, Camilo was allowed to go home on temporary leave to sort out problems with his immigration status. He is a joint Nicaraguan / Costa Rican citizen and only a resident alien in the US. By this time Camilo was having serious doubts about the war and what he was doing in Iraq, and in the stress of combat he turned to God. Already a Catholic, his faith deepened and through that he became profoundly opposed to the war. On the last day of his furlough, Sergeant Mejia decided to ditch the killing and chaos of a conquest gone bad.

For the rest of the autumn and winter he lived like a fugitive, never using cell phones, credit cards or the Internet for fear of being tracked down and busted. He was frequently on the move and survived on the goodwill of friends. The official policy of America's volunteer army is to let deserters go without too much fuss—but better safe than sorry. Dozens of other soldiers also go AWOL, but Mejia is different from most: he plans to make his disobedience into a political protest.

On a cold December afternoon in New York, just before I head back to Iraq for my second trip, I meet Camilo in a small café uptown. He seems tired and stressed but politically clear: "This is an immoral, unjust and illegal war," he says. "The whole thing is based on lies. There are no weapons of mass destruction and there was no link with terrorism. It's about oil, reconstruction contracts and controlling the Middle East."

Over the winter Camilo and I become friends and hang out occasionally: sometimes my girlfriend and I make him dinner at my house, joking about how we're "aiding and abetting a fugitive," or we go to bars in Brooklyn and talk about Iraq. Unlike most US soldiers, Camilo is from a left-wing and bohemian family; his father is Carlos Mejia Godoy, Nicaragua's most famous musician and once the musical laureate of the Sandinista revolution. Camilo was the only kid in his large family who didn't play music, and he was apolitical. "I was a brat. I was a child of the Sandinista elite, and I took politics for granted." After the revolution collapsed, Camilo's mother moved to Miami and so did he. "Suddenly I was a working-class kid, trying to learn English working at Burger King," explains Camilo. "I wanted to become an American, to know the culture, be part of it. So I joined the military—the 3rd ACR."

After four years of active duty Camilo became a reservist and filled his service obligation in the Florida National Guard, which also provided money for college so he could study psychology. Just before Mejia's military service was completed his unit got shipped to Iraq for what was supposed to be a clean, quick war of liberation.

"After the war people were cheering, but within a week or two they were getting angry and asking when we were going to leave. And then it became clear that nothing was getting reconstructed, people's lives weren't getting better. We had all these deadlines for setting up the police, getting the power back on, whatever, and nothing ever got done, nothing changed or got better," Camilo explains. "Then the resistance started."

To make matters worse, Mejia found his officers to be glory-obsessed and intentionally reckless with the safety of their men. In particular, the officers wanted the army's much coveted Combat Infantry Badge—an award bestowed only on those who have met and engaged the enemy.

"To be a twenty-year career infantry officer and not have your CIB is like being a chef and having never cooked or being a fireman and never having put out a fire," says Mejia. "These guys were really hungry, and we were their bait."

In one attempt to draw enemy fire, Mejia's company—about 120 guys divided evenly into four platoons—was ordered to occupy key intersections in Ramadi for several days running. "All the guys were really nervous. This was a total violation of standard operating procedure. They train you to keep moving, not sit in the open." Finally the enemy attacked, and a platoon in Mejia's company took casualties.

When the troops were ordered to perform the same maneuver all over again, Mejia refused. "I told them, I quit." Luckily for him, the four staff sergeants of the platoon that had taken casualties also refused to go out. Technically, refusing an order in a combat situation can be charged as mutiny. But in a tense meeting with their commanding officer the staff sergeants negotiated a new plan of action that allowed the GIs to vary the timing and movement of their patrols. Because of these changes Mejia agreed to go back out.

"We went out two hours earlier than usual and because of that we caught these young guys setting an IED of three mortar shells wrapped together." If Mejia's squad had set out according to the commanding officers' original plan—if there had not been a small rebellion—some of his squad might well have been killed or maimed by that IED.

More disturbing than what Mejia's sociopath officers were doing to him and his comrades were the things that Mejia was forced to do to others. One job involved running a small detention camp. "They didn't call it a POW camp because it didn't meet Red Cross standards," he explained one winter night. "These intelligence guys—I don't know who they were, CIA, DIA or just contractors, there were three of them—they wanted three of the prisoners 'softened up.' That's how they put it. My commanding officer told me to keep the prisoners awake, for like forty-eight hours, or maybe it was longer."

The three resistance suspects, hooded and bound, were locked in tiny metal sheds while Camilo's squad worked in shifts slamming the metal boxes with a sledgehammer around the clock for more than two days. The only breaks from this were occasional mock executions, in which a soldier would press an unloaded pistol against the head of an increasingly disoriented and tormented prisoner and pull the trigger.

"We had one guy lose his mind. He started crying and begging to lie down." When asked how the prisoners were fed and given water, Mejia stares off into space for a minute. Then he says, "I don't remember how we fed them."

When contemplating his fate, Camilo explains that he would rather do the five to ten years in prison for desertion than kill a child by mistake. "When you are getting shot at, you shoot back. It doesn't matter if there are civilians around. Prison ends, but you never get over killing a kid." Camilo is a father, and one of the stories that seems to work at him is the one about a close friend of his who shot a child, a boy of ten who had been carrying a gun.

This soft-spoken young man has plenty of other bad stories as well. There's the time his squad killed a civilian who ran a checkpoint, and the time they shot a demonstrator. There's the officer who forged orders so he could get his unit into combat, and the other officer who broke his own ankle to get out of combat. There is the father who wasn't allowed temporary leave even though his young daughter had been raped. Or there's the story of the GI who took shrapnel in the head and now can't talk, can't take care of himself, can't recognize his family, and wakes up in the middle of the night confused and sobbing.

In every guerrilla war where lack of real reform has lost the battle for hearts and minds—that is, where corruption has fatally undermined attempts to co-opt the insurgency—the government or occupation forces have had to escalate their use of violence. If the proverbial carrot is consumed by the maggots of graft, nepotism and theft, then all that remains is the stick. In that case, separating the "fish" of the guerrilla from the "sea" of the people must become a matter of bombardment, crop destruction, depopulation, forced resettlement and torture. From the American plains of the 1870s to the Philippines of the early 1900s to the Cold War–era conflicts in Vietnam, El Salvador, Guatemala and Colombia, military terror against civilian populations has been the central feature of American counterinsurgency.

In the Iraq war, which unfolds on a media-saturated and largely urbanized terrain, the US faces untested political constraints on the level of the violence it can unleash. This means that in Iraq real reconstruction is even more important than it was in the more rural counterinsurgency campaigns that typified the previous century. In El Salvador and Vietnam the countryside belonged to the guerrillas while the cities were government controlled. In Iraq the insurgency has its bases (or rather lives and operates) in the cities. Can Falluja, Baquba, Najaf, or Baghdad's al-Thawra be treated like the countryside of Vietnam, "drained" of population? Russia has applied such a strategy to Grozny, but the war there goes on.

Urban massacres in Iraq by American troops would massively undermine the already tattered political legitimacy of the United States on the world stage. In short, the US is trapped in a political maze where no path leads to victory.

Considering all these dynamics, it seems that failure is, in fact, America's only option. And when the full history of this bloody circus is written, people will look back slack-jawed at the scale and brazenness of the occupation's corruption and incompetence. History will record Halliburton's colossal greed; the Bush administration's reckless ideological delusions; Paul Bremer's capricious mismanagement; the venality and duplicity of Chalabi, Allawi and the other disobedient, incompetent puppets. And this criminal farce will be visually branded, linked to images of bombed mosques in Falluja, the burning Baghdad library with idle US troops watching, sexual torture and humiliation in Abu Ghraib, and to the swollen skulls of children sick from radiation poisoning.

March 15, 2004, starts with a chilly gray morning. Camilo is going to turn himself in to the military. I drive from New York to the Peace Abbey in Sherborn, Massachusetts, where he will hold a press conference and then surrender. Camilo has hooked up with two activist groups, Citizen Soldier and Military Families Speak Out. Their organizing efforts have brought the press out in force.

At the abbey Camilo is wearing a medallion that has lacquered into it a bit of cloth stained by the blood of the slain Salvadoran Archbishop Oscar Romero. "This is to give me strength," he says as he shows me the talisman.

The questions from the press are insipid but the coverage is good— worldwide. In Nicaragua thousands march in Camilo's honor. The moment when Camilo is cuffed and taken away at the gate of Hanscom Air Force Base west of Boston is awful: the state bares its teeth and swallows my friend.

In the end Camilo is court-martialed at Fort Stewart in Georgia and sentenced to a year in prison. But Camilo bears it like the soldier he is. And in so doing he points the way forward, he connects all the pieces: personal trauma, moral responsibility, and a critique of American empire. Like a soldier, he takes action and makes sacrifices in the interest of others. And like all soldiers he will pay a dear price, but this time his fight is just and worth the cost.

Meanwhile, Saddam is gone and that is good, but much of Iraq spirals toward greater chaos or perhaps a return to brutal despotism. Where it will all end is impossible to say, but for Iraq and the Middle East as a whole this war has been a tragedy of staggering proportions. It has directly caused immeasurable damage and indirectly unleashed irredentist and fundamentalist dynamics that are already playing out in horrifically brutal ways. Perhaps the only aspect of the current crisis that is remotely positive is that the official vision of Planet America, run by bullying from Washington, is beginning to dissolve like a bad hallucination ebbing away.

Notes

Chapter 1

1 There is a long literature on Iraq's development. For a discussion of Saddam's role, see Said K. Aburish, *Saddam Hussein: The Politics of Revenge* (London: Bloomsbury 2000).

2 James Kelly, "Battling for the Advantage; France Sends Fighter-Bombers to Iraq, Adding a New Dimension to a Risky War," *Time*, October 24, 1983.

3 John Greenwald, "The Cartel Is Losing Its Clout," *Time*, January 3, 1983; Charles P. Alexander, "The Humbling of OPEC," *Time*, February 7, 1983; George F. Will, "The Blessings of Cheap Oil," *Washington Post*, January 22, 1989.

4 Dilip Hiro, *The Longest War: The Iran–Iraq Military Conflict* (London: Routledge 1989), p. 250.

5 Craig Unger, *House of Bush, House of Saud: The Secret Relationship Between the World's Two Most Powerful Dynasties* (New York: Scribner's 2004): p. 69, p. 83; see also pp. 65–70 and 73–82.

6 Roger Vielvoye, "Iraq-Kuwait Border Dispute," *Oil and Gas Journal*, May 6, 1991.

7 Kamal Taha, "Iraqi Children the First and Worst to Be Hit under Sanctions," Agence France-Presse, August 16, 1999; "Iraq Surveys Show 'Humanitarian Emergency,'" UNICEF press release, August 12, 1999.

8 BBC Monitoring, Middle East, June 25, 2003 (page unavailable online), 2003 WL 58748487. "Over 1,000 Palestinians Said Stranded in Camp on Jordan–Iraq border."

9 Wire Reports, *Florida Sun-Sentinel*, April 22, 2003.

Chapter 2

1 Jeffrey Fleishman, "Back into Baghdad's Streets," *Los Angeles Times*, January 22, 2004.

2 Matthew McAllester, "In Iraq, It's Law vs. Law: Tribal Justice Prevalent in Absence of Strong Police Force," *Newsday*, February 1, 2004.

3 Dexter Filkins, "US Forces Employing Israeli-style Tactics," New York Times News Service, December 7, 2003.

4 Panel discussion by Middle East Policy Council in Washington, October 3, 2003; State Department Press Releases and Documents, October 3, 2003. (

5 U.N. Commission on Human Rights, "Integration of the Human Rights of Women and the Gender Perspective," (E/CN.4/2002/83), January 31, 2002, para. 23.)

6 Abdalrahman al-Juburi and Zaid H. Fahmi "Sectarianism 101: Intolerance and Tensions on the Rise at Baghdad Universities," Iraq Today, March 22, 2004.

Chapter 3

1 Rajiv Chandrasekaran, "Attacks Force Retreat from Wide-Ranging Plans for Iraq," Washington Post, December 29, 2003.

2 Bryan Rouke, "Author Accused of Smuggling Iraqi Artifacts," Providence Journal, October 13, 2003.

3 "Cheney Left Halliburton Holding Asbestos Bag," Cincinnati Enquirer, September 2, 2002.

4 Nomi Prins, "Iraq Could Produce Another Enron," Newsday, December 2, 2003; "Squandering the Future," Columbus Dispatch, May 3, 2004.

5 Matt Kelley, "10 US Contractors in Iraq Penalized," Associated Press, April 26, 2004.

6 Mary Pat Flaherty and Jackie Spinne, "GAO Cites Cost Risks in Undefined Iraq Contracts," Washington Post, April 28, 2004, p. A15.

7 Pratap Chatterjee and Herbert Docena, "Occupation, Inc.," Southern Exposure, Winter 2003/2004 (http://www.southernstudies.org/reports/OccupationInc.htm).

8 Dahr Jamail, "Iraq's Only Disabilities Hospital Desperately Underfunded, Inaccessible," The New Standard (online), April 29, 2004: http://newstandardnews.net/content/?action=show_item&itemid=251&printmode=true.

9 Nigel Morris, "Iraq Crisis: Rise in Birth Deformities Blamed on Allies' Deadly Weaponry," Independent, May 13, 2004.

Chapter 5

1 BBC monitoring of the statement.

2 Quoted in Mark Mazzetti, "Finishing the Job," US News & World Report, December 29, 2003.

3 Nicholas Blandford, "Insurgent Speaks Out on Anti-US Attacks in Fallujah," Daily Star, February 14, 2004.

4 "In Fedayeen's Path, Long-Term Plans, Unlikely Organization," Iraq Today, December 29, 2003. Even Mao saw the military as one of the main sources of his guerrilla army:

The second type of guerrilla unit is that which is organized from small units of the regular forces temporarily detached for the purpose. For example, since hostilities commenced, many groups have been temporarily detached from armies, divisions, and brigades and have been assigned guerrilla duties... The third type of unit consists of a detachment of regulars who are permanently assigned guerrilla duties. This type of small detachment does not have to be prepared to rejoin the regular forces. Its post is somewhere in the rear of the enemy, and there it becomes the backbone of guerrilla organization. (*On Guerrilla Warfare*)

5 Sudarsan Raghavan and Jonathan S. Landay, "US Soldiers Raid City Looking for Resistance Fighters," *Bradenton Herald,* December 18, 2003.

6 Thom Shanker, "Saddam's Secret Service Planned for Insurgency, Pentagon Finds," *New York Times/International Herald Tribune,* April 30, 2004.

7 Scott Ritter, "Defining the Resistance in Iraq: It's Not Foreign and It's Well Prepared," *Christian Science Monitor,* November 10, 2003.

8 Greg Mills, "Why the US Loses More Troops in Iraq," *Chicago Tribune,* March 14, 2004.

9 Denis D. Gray, "US Military Shifts Tactics with Iraqis," Associated Press, April 5, 2004.

Chapter 6

1 James Hider, "Iraq's Leaky Border with Iran," *Christian Science Monitor,* August 27, 2003.

Chapter 7

1 "Suicide Bomber Wounds Three Guards of Iraqi Tribal Chief," Agence France-Presse, February 10, 2004

2 Ellen Knickmeyer, "US Forces Return Fire at Iraq Protest," Associated Press, April 29, 2003.

3 Alex Berenson, "US Troops Kill 8 Iraqi Policemen by Mistake," *New York Times/International Herald Tribune,* September 13, 2003.

4 Patrick J. McDonnell, "US Adopts New Tactics to Counter Iraqi Foes," *Los Angeles Times,* September 7, 2003.

5 "ICDC Fights Off Iraqi Insurgents, Task Force All American Assists," Release 040215f, Cjtf-7 Coalition Press Information Center, Feb. 15, 2004, Baghdad, Iraq.

6 "COMEX Gold Turns Higher on Iraqi Bombing Reports," Reuters, Wednesday, April 7, 2004.